# The Caballero from Catalonia

# The Caballero
## from Catalonia

## The Life of Juan Duval

### Joseph A. Bonelli

SUNSTONE
PRESS

SANTA FE

Sunstone books may be purchased for educational, business, or sales promotional use.
For information please write: Special Markets Department, Sunstone Press,
P.O. Box 2321, Santa Fe, New Mexico 87504-2321.

Book and cover design › Vicki Ahl
Body typeface › Goudy Old Style
Printed on acid-free paper

∞

—————————

Library of Congress Cataloging in Publication Control Number: 2018026454

Names: Bonelli, Joseph A., 1942- author.
Title: The caballero from Catalonia : the life of Juan Duval / by Joseph A.
    Bonelli.
Description: Santa Fe : Sunstone Press, [2018]
Identifiers: LCCN 2018026454 | ISBN 9781632932341 (softcover : alk. paper)
Subjects: LCSH: Duval, Juan. | Entertainers~Spain~Biography.
Classification: LCC PN2788.D88 B66 2018 | DDC 792.092 [B] ~dc23
LC record available at https://lccn.loc.gov/2018026454

—————————

**WWW.SUNSTONEPRESS.COM**
SUNSTONE PRESS / POST OFFICE BOX 2321 / SANTA FE, NM 87504-2321 /USA
(505) 988-4418 / ORDERS ONLY (800) 243-5644 / FAX (505) 988-1025

# Dedication

To the people of Catalonia—in this their time of travail.

# CONTENTS

## 5
## Juan's Legacy / 87

## Selected References / 104

# Acknowledgements

To my wife Joyce whose fifty-plus years of marriage to me, make her a participant in some of the events of this narrative. And whose awesome insights into the human psyche enabled me to understand the far past of my own childhood.

To my granddaughter Samantha Bonelli who found John Duval for me on the Internet and who assisted me with historical research; and to my son, Damon Bonelli, who also assisted with Internet research.

# Preface

Juan Duval (Juan Bellavista Xicart) was born in Barcelona, the heart of Catalonia, in 1897. He was a man of action and artistry in four worlds. He made a career for himself first in his native Spain. Later, when he went to Paris and London he assumed the stage name "Juan Duval" and retained this for his career in Latin America and the Anglo world of the U.S.

Juan Duval.

How highly he was regarded in Spain back in 1934 is indicated in following by Federico Garcia Lorca:

"Júan Duval, one of the greatest poets of twentieth century Spain, was born in Barcelona, of a middle-class family of Gypsy origin. From the age of fifteen he had been writing lyrical verses of an extraordinarily original and striking kind, based mostly on the forms and idioms of Andalusian folk lore. These earlier poems of his were not published until 1924, but a volume of his mature verse called 'Gitanerias' appeared in 1917. It was soon followed by a play in two acts, 'CLAVELES ROJOS,' then poems y *Canciones del Cante Hondo.*

"His works, highly praised by the late Vicente Blasco Ibañes, Antonio Machado, Manuel de Falla, Antonio Triana, and one of the greatest of composers, Francisco Avellan, encouraged him to write 'Sombras Gitanas,' a musical drama, which played in every province and city of Spain, from 1934 to 1936.

"This great play so inspired Senor Francisco Avellan to the extent that he wrote his masterpiece."

In Spain he was a friend of famous composers Manuel de Falla, and Francisco Avellan; dancers Triana and La Argentina. He tried, though unsuccessfully to steer his friend Federico Garcia Lorca out of harm's way at the beginning of the Spanish Civil War. In America he was a friend of famous ventriloquist Señor Wences, Jose and Amparo Iturbi, concert pianists of worldwide fame; Emilio Osta, child musical prodigy and concert pianist, Victor Granados (son of Enrique), actors John McIntyre, Warner Anderson, and many others who were part of that period of Hollywood.

He had a reputation in the Hispanic world of Mexico, Cuba, Argentina, and Brazil. He was a man of multiple talents: a dancer, (Spanish-Gypsy, French-Apache); a choreographer, and a director/producer of musical revues and movies. He was a poet, linguist, a soldier in two World Wars and the Foreign Legion, and a businessman. He was a musician (piano) and composer. A friend of bullfighters. He ran his own Spanish dance school on Hollywood Boulevard. He was a model stepfather and husband. A Hollywood character actor and screenwriter. A writer, amateur historian, and playwright. In short, he was a Renaissance man!

Juan was also a Caballero, un Chevalier, a Gentleman of the Old School. Someone worth remembering.

Juan Duval was my stepfather. I knew Juan first when I was a child of five, but six-and-a-half years later he exited my life after a painful bout with cancer. The chronology of life events I've put together here is the best that can be picked out and recollected from a child's memory, pieces of scrapbooks, and some Internet news clippings. Objective confirmation of precise dates and events is seldom possible. Often family photos were unlabeled or undated. Juan didn't write diaries, collect legal papers, or have a publicist. He just lived!

Geo-politically, Juan was born a Catalan and Spaniard, was made a temporary French citizen by the Great War, and became a U.S. citizen by serving in the U.S. Armed Forces at the end of World War I and the beginning of World War II. Juan used his talents as writer and poet in Spain in 1937—in support of the Republican cause, at constant risk of his life.

Today's readers will like Juan when they read of a multi-talented artist who was not twisted or conflicted, but a decent human being and an old-fashioned Gentleman. Today's myth of the artist as demented genius could use some debunking.

—Joseph A. Bonelli, Stepson of Juan Duval
(Amateur Historian by virtue of "Being There")

# 1

# Childhood and Early Adulthood, 1897–1926

Juan Bellavista Xicart was born in Barcelona on April 28, 1897, to a middle-class traditional Spanish family. His father was a fisherman who owned his own boat and made a good living from it; enough to see his son well-educated. Juan had two sisters. Ignacia, the youngest, was born around 1903. His other sister (name unknown) was probably older.

First photograph of Juan, circa 1906 with sister Ignacia.

Both sisters became nuns. The oldest became a "discalced" (barefoot) Carmelite and lived in a convent with strict vows of silence. Ignacia joined an order of nuns who worked among the poor and were less austere regarding rules for dress.

According to Federico Garcia Lorca, who was a good friend of Juan's, Juan was "of Gypsy origin." I don't know if that was the strict truth or artistic license. It may have been a sort of artistic encomium; he had the heart and soul and talent of a Gypsy musician. In any case, Juan was writing gypsy verse as a teenager and as an adult was fluent in the Gypsy language, in Catalan, Spanish, French, Portuguese, Italian, and English.

In 1915 Juan earned a PhD from Montserrat University/Monastery outside of Barcelona in the Spanish Language and Literature. Afterward he wandered through Andalusia for a time, and then went to Paris later that year to study rudiments of classical dancing with a view to later interpretation of the Spanish classical dances. Paris was then viewed as the world capital of culture, particularly for artists and intellectuals. That is why he went and changed his last name to "Duval."

He was attracted also by France's democratic and egalitarian principles, and its openness to new ideas. By contrast, his beloved Spain at the time was mired in political confusion and social backwardness.

In 1916 he was conscripted into the French Foreign Legion and sent to Tunis, North Africa. At the time he still held a Spanish passport so he shared the same fate as many foreigners who were living in France at the time.

At this point he was either let out of the Legion to join the French Infantry for the latter part of the Battle of Verdun or participated in that battle as a Legionnaire. In any case, he was there for this epic but horrifying battle and got facial wounds and a dose of poison gas which was used by the Germans there in warfare for the first time.

According to historian Paul K. Davis in *100 Decisive Battles from Ancient Times to the Present*, Verdun was the key symbolic battle of World War I. French morale was lifted by the rallying cry of the French defenders, "They shall not pass!"

According to Davis' brief description of the battle the Germans used phosgene gas (which is invisible). Juan said he got hit by "mustard gas" (which is visible). Possibly the Germans used both in that battle or Juan got the mustard gas at a different time on a different part of the front.

In 1917 Juan connected with and enlisted into the U.S. Army. I don't know exactly how this happened. My guess is the French Army found it useful to pass along to their American allies an experienced soldier who was fluent both in French and English (and not a French citizen). At this point his linguistic abilities might have gotten him off the front lines.

Thus he served with the U.S. Army (50th Infantry) in France, and later in Germany near the Rhine with the Army of Occupation. Despite the war, he managed to get a book of poems *Gitanerias* published in 1917. *Gitanerias* translates loosely to "playful Gypsy song/verse." This was followed by a play in two acts, *Claveles Rojos* ("Red Carnations"); then poems and canciones *Del Cante Hondo* ("Deep Song"). "Canciones" are songs, and "Cante Hondo" is what we call flamenco.

In 1919 he came to the United States and worked as a choreographer for New York's Metropolitan Opera, touring South America until 1921.

In 1924 his early poems on Andalusia and Gypsy folklore were published.

Following is the oldest poem of Juan's in this book. It's a humorous "love poem" written in Barcelona in 1924, in a lyrical and literate Spanish. In the last part of the poem there is a Gypsy speech pattern (dropping d's out of words, such a "dao" for "dado," "lao" for "lado," etc.). This poem deserves a better translation from poetic scholars than I can give it.

Juan never translated any of his poems from Spanish to English. All such translations throughout this work are mine.

## MARINOCHE

*Sacude el viento los troncos*
*Y las hojas se mantienen,*
*En los olivos que aguarda*
*La moza de tez morena.*
*Mientras chillan las campanas*
*For el viento que las sopla,*
*volando ondulan mis piernas*
*Sin rumbo mi cuerpo llevan.*
*La negrura de la noche*
*Que ilumina el riochuelo,*
*Hace que entre los olivos*
*Oiga una voz, de consuelo.*
*La moza de tez morena*
*Que al verme grita de espanto,*
*Marinoche, marinoche, Ay!*
*Llenan sus Senos gitanos.*
*Me devuelve la sonrisa*

Y el marfil entre sus labios,
Como una estrella ilumina
Su tez de Olivo Murano.
Enfocamos los Luceros
De hito en hito fascinados,
Y nuestros labios se miran
Boca a boca, labio a labio,
Sopla el viento y nos caemos
Sobre la hierba rosada,
Y su cuerpo enciende el mio
Y encadenan nuestros brazos.
Crecen sus redondos senos
De mi pecho aprisionados,
Y sus caderas Gitanas
Ritma con toda la gracia.
El Alba que apunta el dia
Aduerme el viento con calma,
Crece el verde en los olivos
Y el Sol viene a saludarnos.

Riochelo que testigo
Entre corriente te vas,
De una noche Marinoche
De.un idilio pasional.
Despedirme no esperaba
No sin verla más y más,
Moziya de tez morena
Vaya chasco el que me das.
Casi me caigo de espaldas
Cuando a su vez me soltó
No me das una estampiya
Como el pare confesor.
La mire sus ojos negros
Y su boca pasional,
Me acaricio de un mordizco
Todo lo que Dios me Ha dao.
Marinoche, Marinoche, Ay!

Me sollozó una vez mas,
U me das una estampiya
U no me confiesas mas.
La implore que me esperara
Mas me solto el temporal,
Y cruzando el Riochuelo
Me dejo muy bien plantao.
Marinoche, Marinoche,
Me grito del otro lao:
Mi confesor es ma Gueno
Porque despues del bocao,
Dentro mi corpiño mete
Lo que tanto me has negao,

Una estampa de colores,
For haberme confesao.

Marinoche, Marinoche,
Vaya chasco me he llevao.

Por
JUAN DUVAL
Barcelona 1924

# 2

# Dancing, Writing, Choreography, and Movie Acting Careers, 1926–1936

In January of 1926, Juan was in the midst of his dancing career. Here is a souvenir photograph of Antonia Merce (La Argentina) one of the most famous female Spanish dancers of that time.

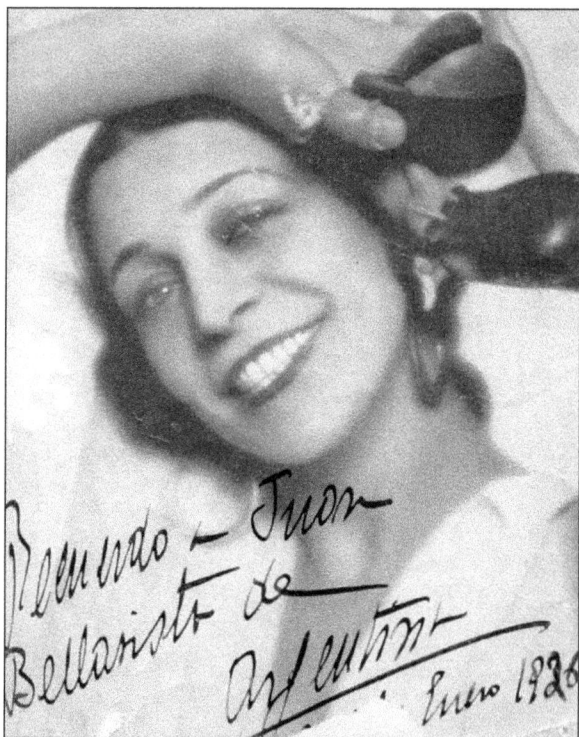

Antonia Merce.

Juan also danced with other celebrities of the day, Carmen Amaya and Pastora Imperio. In the next two photographs, Juan's partners are not identified.

In 1926, Juan directed the Spanish-language movie *El Precio De Un Beso* in Hollywood. Juan was director of choreography for "One Mad Kiss," a talking 1929 Hollywood movie made by Fox Studios. It was probably around this time he opened his studio of Spanish Dance on Hollywood Boulevard and advertised with this brochure.

**JUAN DUVAL**
Spanish Studio of Dancing
6422 Hollywood Blvd.          Phone Granite 7995
Room 201 ~ 202 Across from Warner Bros. Theatre

## Come and See Come Now
**ORIGINAL     DIFERENT     FINISHED**

MUSIC BY
DE FALLA
GRANADOS
ALBENIZ
GUERRERO
M. INFANTE
G. VALVERDE
G. DURAN
M. RAVEL
TURINA
J. LACREGLA
ALL FROM
SPAIN
SPECIAL TECH
NIQUE OF
CASTANET
PLAYING AND
HEEL
DANCING

THE ROU-
TINES AND
TECHNIQUE
TAUGHT HERE
ARE THE SAME
AS ARE
TAUGHT IN
SPAIN
BY THE
FAMOUS OTE-
RO - ROMAN
REALITO
VIDAL
ESCUDERO
JUAN DUVAL
FROM
BARCELONA
SPAIN
OF REAL
SPANISH
DANCING
MORISH AND
GIPSY DANCES

**JUAN DUVAL**
**Stage Director, Actor Teacher**
PRODUCER OF CAVE OF SORROWS PLAY, LILA MUSICAL
COMEDY, SPANISH LOVE, DRAMA, CAFE MADRID, REVUE,
SPANISH REVUE, AND NIGTH IN PARIS DRAMA.

**Front of brochure.**

## I Shall Mention the Most Famous Dancers

the later Isidora Duncan

the later Mata Hari

the later Cabby Desli

Tortola Valencia

Antonia Merce, La Argentina

Both of them great Dancers

"Why, it is simply because they have studied just the art of their dancing, and the reason that today we don't see great dancers is because girls don't study enough. They try to do to many things at once singing dancing of all kinds, and finally they accomplish none of those to perfection.          THAT'S WHY

## My way of Teaching will Satisfy You and Convince your PRODUCER'S

THAT MEAN WORK SUCCESS MONEY

I Came from Barcelona, Spain, 1912

Performing with my uncle M. Duval, my master - considered a genius unique for all his shows were his own died in Paris in 1918. We played in Spain, France, Italy, England, Germany, Belgium, and South America.

## My Work in America

I came to America in 1918 from Paris, France with engagement at Winter Garden Passing Show in

1920 Apollo Theatre, Buenos Aires — Argentine

1921 Casino Thearte, Rio de Janeiro — Brasil

1922-23 Carrol Theatre, New York, The Gingham Girl

1924 Palace Theatre, N.Y. Humming Bird

1925 Picadilly and Kit-Kat, London, England

1926 Music Box Theatre — Hollywood, Revue

1927 I staged Cafe Madrid — Cave of Sorrows

1928-29 Publix Theatres — Parisienne Nights—Revue

## And now to Show Hollywood a new Creation of Spanish Ensembles

Inside of brochure.

Thus began his career in the Hollywood movie industry and the Golden State. San Francisco, and particularly its opera house, was part of the attraction, and perhaps, like millions of others, California's lovely climate, and Los Angeles before the smog. Juan's work still took him around much of the world, but from this point on Hollywood was his home base.

In 1930, he directed *El Sol de Mexico* in Spanish, in Mexico.

**Photograph of Juan's entire family taken around 1930.**

The nun in the habit is his older sister. Ignacia is in the middle. The presence of the older sister suggests this was a very special occasion; cloistered Carmelites were seldom allowed by their abbess to visit their family of origin. Some human and church politics lie behind the scenes here.

Juan's father nearly drowned when his fishing boat sunk. He had no insurance or savings to replace it, and when Juan learned of this Juan bought his father a new boat! The Church felt this act of Christian generosity was good reason to give the older sister a pass to be with the rest of the family to celebrate. Perhaps they hoped Juan would be a benefactor to the Church someday. Alas, he died broke, but with no debts.

This photograph, taken by Juan, of a group of his friends in Barcelona in 1931 is top heavy with famous artists of the day. This confirms his dancing career was doing well at this time.

The two women on the left, Carmela and Manuela, were probably dance partners or friends of Juan. Manuela says, "Ole, you are more Spanish than Calderon," (a famous Spanish writer). Carmela says, "Juanito, you are my inspiration." The man on the right is the famous dancer Antonio Triana and he says, "Juan Duval, the most noble of all the Gypsies." One of the other men, I think the shorter on the left, is Manuel de Falla, probably the most famous Spanish composer alive at the time. He says, "For the artist and great poet, Juan Duval, as a remembrance of your friend. M. de Falla, Barcelona, 1931." Manuel de Falla was a "caballero" and history records what he bravely tried to do for another friend in 1936. But that's getting ahead of the story. It's possible the other man is Francisco Avellan, the composer.

Juan was a bullfighting aficionado and highly knowledgeable on the subject. One of the few books he kept at home was Hemingway's classic, *Death in the Afternoon*.

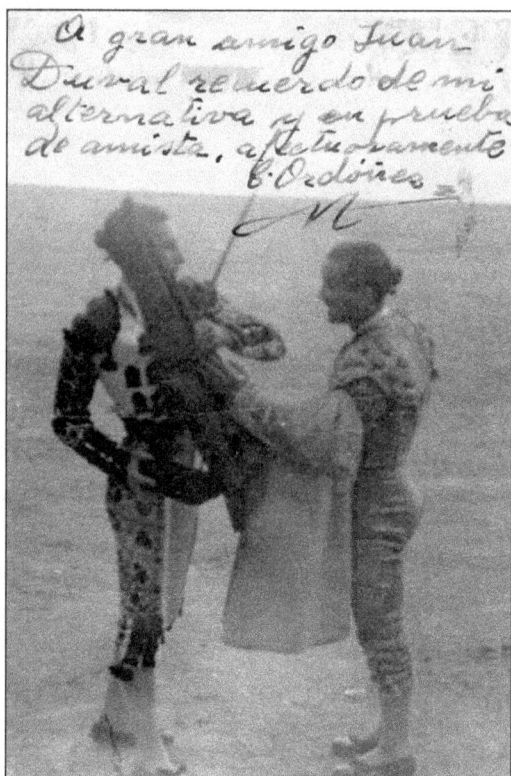

This photograph is inscribed to Juan by the famous bullfighter Ordoñez who was a friend of his.

What other books did Juan keep around the house besides *Death in the Afternoon?* Carl Jung's *Modern Man in Search of a Soul, L'Atalant* (a book in Catalan about fabled Atlantis), *Don Gaucho* by Alyce Pollock, a personal friend of Juan's, inscribed by the author to "Juan and Carmen, February, 1950," and (in Spanish) *El Patio De Los Naranjos* by Hernandez Mir. That last book Juan used mostly as one of my reading primers to help me learn to read and write Spanish at home.

Sometime in the early 1930s Juan began to appear as an extra, and in small parts in Hollywood movies, including a few Westerns.

Juan shown with Fred Astaire and Ginger Rogers in 1933s "Flying Down to Rio,"
their first pairing.

This movie "still" is from an old Western. If you know the movie's name or year, you're a
better movie historian than I am!

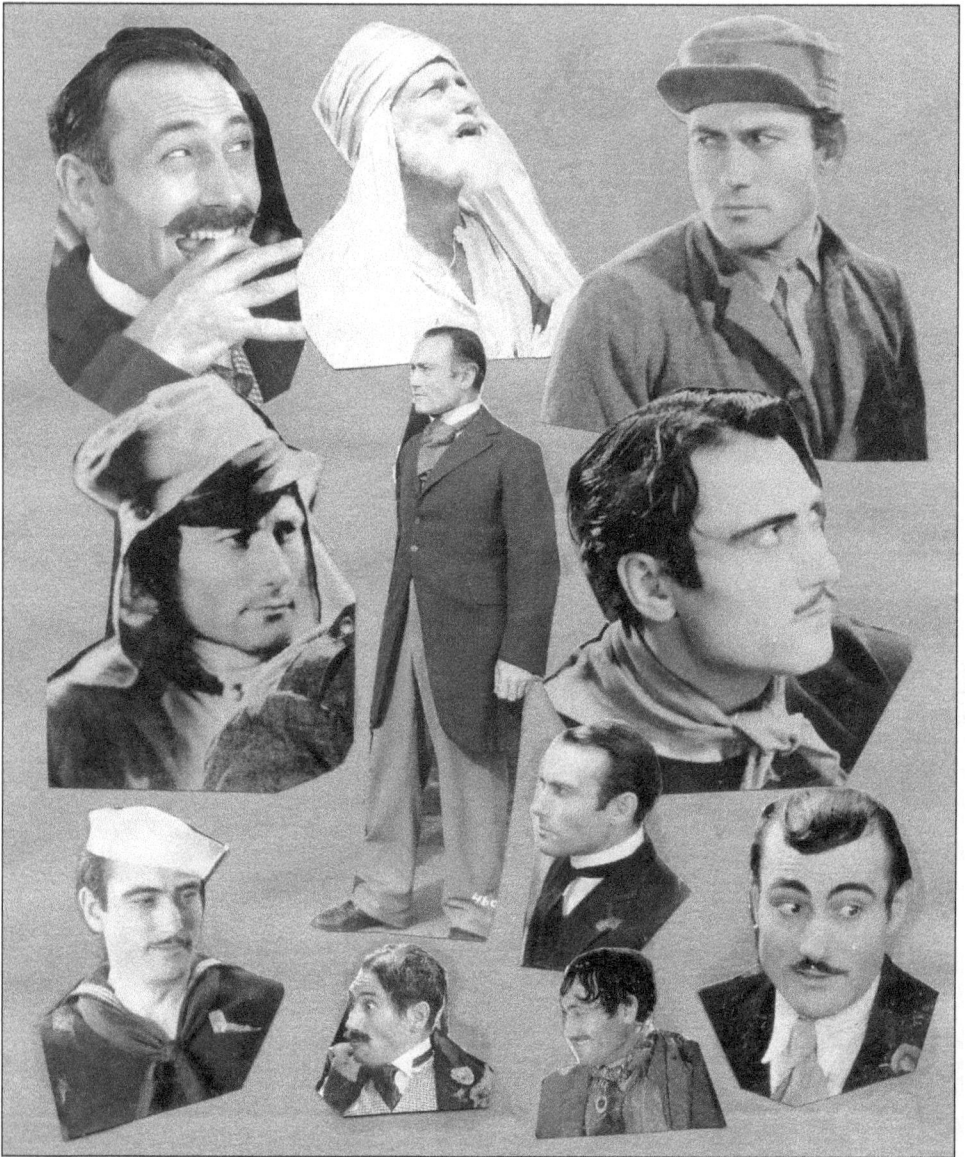

A simple collage/composite of many of Juan's roles. He had a handsome and expressive face, which the camera liked, and could change his facial expressions and personality at will.

Juan himself created this collage, trimming the images from some old photographs and creatively composing this grouping. Perhaps he even provided it to his agent to help him get more roles. If you study this collage you can see why Juan was in such demand in Hollywood for character actor roles. He could be made up to be almost anybody—an Arab, a legionnaire, a sailor, a gentleman, and all with little or no makeup or props. At first glance it's hard to believe all these images are the same actor. But they are.

In the old days actors could receive (or perhaps pay for) "stills" which are simply photographs taken on the set by still cameramen. Therefore each of these images is like an archival record of a movie role Juan completed.

Juan's poem below, *Sardinerita Ya Vengo* ("Lovely Little Sardine Maid, I'm Coming"), is a sad, poignant poem of a fisherman who does not come home, written like *Marinoche* in an elegant and lyrical Spanish but without Gypsy speech patterns. Given its subject matter, I conjecture it was written after 1930 and his father's near drowning. In it Juan shows a surprising technical knowledge of how a sailing ship is built, and how it is properly sailed.

## SARDINERITA YA VENGO

*!Playa playita playera!*
*cantan los mozos bogando*
*desafiando las olas*
*por la corriente arrastradas.*

*Noche de claro de Luna*
*para la pesca ideal*
*la vela mayor descienden*
*ya han parado de bogar.*

*!Playa playita playera!*
*cantan los mozos pescando,*
*las sardinas prisioneras*
*Van subiendo a toneladas.*

*Ya el patron les da su mando,*
*los mozos suben la vela;*
*el timonero se cuadra*
*y pone a rumbo el barcuelo.*

!Playa playita playera!
que en alta mar navegando,
lYa vengo Sardinerita!
Alegres los mozos cantan.

Sale el Sol rojo y bravio,
saludando por la popa:
Y el viento sopla furioso
sin piedad nuestra barquilla.

Las olas del norte ondulan;
Agitadas por el viento,
Y el mar forma sus. montanas
altas como el firmamento.

!Playa playita playera! Nadie habla, rie u llora,
uno murmura rezando!
Sardinerita ya vengo!

La tarde obscura y nublada,
navega a flote el barquillo,
partiendo el pecho a las olas,
que estrellan sobre el estribo.

Con el Aspa aclibillada,
y ha pedazos la menor,
entra arrogante el navio
en la playa que salio.

El pueblo esperando esta:
ansioso de ver los suyos.
Con el farol en la mano,
piloteando el barquillo.

El patron con alta voz,
da mando de dar al fondo

ya el barquillo llego a puerto.
Sardinerita ya vengo!

Mas unos ojos bañados
y una voz en llanto grita,
por el mozo que cantaba
ya vengo Sardinerita!

Uno a uno van bajando,
a tierra los pescadores,
pero nadie le contesta
Sardinerita ya vengo!

La playa esta desolada!
Inquieta sigue la noche,
las olas furiosas rompen
sobre las desnudas rocas.

!Playa playita playera!
Donde el mozo pescador,
en noches de clara Luna
cantaba alegre su amor.

Con el pelo alborotado
y la falda a medio cuerpo
la Sardinerita espera,
al hombre que ella mas quiere.

El Alba ya apunta al dia,
el mar sereno ha calmado.
y a lo lejos ella escucha
!Playa playita playera!
Sardinerita ya vengo!

–Por JUAN DUVAL

## LOVELY LITTLE SARDINE MAID—I'M COMING

Seacoast, little beach, fisherwoman!
Sing the young men rowing
Challenging the waves
By the current swept backwards

A clear night of Moon
Ideal for fishing
The mainsail comes down
Already they've stopped rowing

Seacoast, little beach, fisherwoman!
Sing the young men fishing
The sardine prisoners
Come upwards by the ton

The captain gives his order
The young men hoist the sail
The helmsman faces to quarter
And sets the little barque on course

Seacoast, little beach, fisherwoman!
Who with high seas navigate
I'm coming lovely little sardine maid
Sing the young men happily

Out comes the Sun red and brave
Greeting from the poopdeck
And the wind rushes furiously
without pity upon our little boat

The waves of the north undulate
Agitated by the wind
And the ocean forms it's mountains
high like the firmament

Seacoast, little beach, fisherwoman!
No one speaks, laughs or cries
A prayerful murmuring
Lovely little Sardine Maid—I'm coming!

The afternoon is dark and foggy
The little boat is still afloat
Baring it's breast against the waves
Which batter against the keel buttresses

With the Bentinck shrouds smashed
And with lost pieces a smaller ship
The sailing vessel jauntily enters
The port from which it sailed

The whole town expecting her
Anxious to see their own
With a lantern in hand
They pilot the little boat

The captain with a loud voice
Gives the order to drop anchor
And the barque arrives in port
Lovely little Sardine Maid—I'm coming!
Under eyes washed with tears
And one voice in grief cries
For the young man who sang
Lovely little Sardine Maid—I'm Coming!

One by one they descend
The fisherman to the shore
But no one answers her back
Lovely little Sardine Maid—I'm Coming!

The beach is deserted!
Unsettled is the night
The furious waves break
Upon the bare rocks.

Seacoast, little beach, fisherwoman!
Where the young fisherman
In nights of clear Moon
Sung happily his love.

With her hair disheveled
And her skirt held tight against her
The lovely little Sardine Maid waits
For the man she loves the most

The Dawn now marks the day
The ocean serene has calmed
And far off, she hears
Seacoast, little beach, fisherwoman!
Lovely little Sardine Maid, I'm Coming!

As mentioned earlier, in the early thirties, Manuel de Falla, Antonio Triana, and one of Spain's greatest composers, Francisco Avellan, encouraged Juan to write *Sombras Gitanas* ("Gypsy Shadows"), a musical drama which played in every province and city of Spain from 1934 to 1936.

This great dramatization inspired Avellan to compose the musical score for it, which became his musical masterpiece. Avellan and Duval toured with "Gypsy Shadows."

The following playbill (from a later 1940 performance in San Francisco) is presented to give the reader a feeling of what "Gypsy Shadows" was about; a blending of dance, music, and theater.

UNION ESPAÑOLA
PRESENTS
THE GREATEST SPANISH MUSICAL PLAY OF THE GENERATION, IN 3 ACTS
## "GYPSY SHADOWS"
Direct from Spain, London, Paris, and South America.

# Sombras Gitanas

Juan Duval
AUTHOR

MUSICA DE
Francisco Avellan

Presentan
CARMEN
ESTRABEAU
Con
LA TROUPE DE.....
GRANADA, SPAIN
Director
JUAN DUVAL

NATIVE SONS AUDITORIUM
Mason Street bet. Post and Geary
Saturday, Nov. 2, and Sunday, Nov. 3, 1940—8:15 p. m.
PRICES $1.50—$1.00—50c

TICKETS AT SHERMAN & CLAY AND AT ST. FRANCIS HOTEL NEWS STAND

35

## "GYPSY SHADOWS"

*By* Juan Duval and Francisco Avellan

*Program*

SINFONIA—"A MORNING IN GRANADA"

### CAST

| | |
|---|---|
| SOLEA—Gitana | CARMEN ESTRABEAU |
| NICO—GYPSY | DANTON FERRERO |
| FELIPE—ARISTOCRAT | JOSE L. TORTOSA |
| MANOLIN—GYPSY | MANOLO ALDA |
| D. FERNANDO—MARQUES | CARLOS VILLARIAS |
| PEPIN—GYPSY | PEPE RODRIGUEZ |
| JOSELIYO—MATADOR | JUAN ROMERO |
| PADRE—FRAILE | MANUEL SANGUEZA |
| ROSARIO—MARQUESITA | CELESTE SAVOI |

### Music and Dances

**First Act**

| | |
|---|---|
| En la Tierra é Graná | Soleá and Gypsies |
| Gitana me Yaman | Soleá and Gypsies |
| Noche Morena Moruna | Soleá |

**Second Act**

| | |
|---|---|
| Boca boca labio a labio | Soleá |
| Flores y Toreros | Gypsies |

**Third Act**

| | |
|---|---|
| Malas Lenguas Fandanguillos | Soleá |
| Guitarras Morunas | Soleá and Nico |
| A Night in Sevilla | Soleá and Gypsies |

Music by Francisco Avellan
Lyrics by Juan Duval

### Comments

Francisco Avellan, one of the greatest composers, pianists and conductors of the 20th century, in Spain, was born at Valencia. In his early days he studied with Granados and received the greatest honors in the Conservatory of Music of Valencia. Today he is being praised by his close friend and fellow student, José Iturbi, for his mastery and complete understanding of the Gypsy school of melody, the tradition and rhythmic perfection of which were lost.

The greatest masters, once his teachers, have paid homage to his skill and daring in reviving the Gypsy music and enhancing its beauty. Today Francisco Avellan is the outstanding creator and performer of this beautiful school of music, as exemplified in "Gypsy Shadows."

VICENTE ESCUDERO.
PARTORA IMPERIO.
ANTONIA MERCE
(La Argentina).

Júan Duval, one of the greatest poets of twentieth century Spain, was born in Barcelona, of a middle-class family of Gypsy origin. From the age of fifteen he had been writing lyrical verses of an extraordinarily original and striking kind, based mostly on the forms and idioms of Andalusian folk lore. These earlier poems of his were not published until 1924, but a volume of his mature verse called "Gitanerias" appeared in 1917. It was soon followed by a play in two acts, "CLAVELES ROJOS"; then poems y Canciones del Cante Hondo.

His works, highly praised by the late Vicente Blasco Ibañes, Antonio Machado, Manuel de Fella, Antonio Triana, and one of the greatest of composers, Francisco Avellan, encouraged him to write "Sombras Gitanas," a musical drama, which played in every province and city of Spain, from 1934 to 1936.

This great play so inspired Señor Francisco Avellan to the extent that he wrote his masterpiece. Both Avellan and Duval are touring with "Gypsy Shadows."

FEDERICO GARCIA LORCA.

---

Juan, like his friend Señor Wences, the famous ventriloquist, had considerable talent in drawing and caricature. His profile (below the "SO" in the playbill) is Juan's own self-portrait.

From 1934 to 1936, Juan and *Sombras Gitanas* were doing well touring Spain, but then something terrible changed all that, the onset of the Spanish Civil War, one of the most awful chapters of 20th century history.

# 3

# The Spanish Civil War, 1936–1937

Just before the outbreak of the war, Juan met his old friend Federico Garcia Lorca in Lyon, France. I'll let Juan tell you this story in his own words:

In the summer of 1936 I met my old friend Federico Garcia Lorca, in Lyon, France. I learned that he had just arrived from Mexico with his own musical folk-lore, "La Barraca." After dismissing his Gypsy Company he wanted to have a few weeks of rest and travel throughout "Le Midi."

Lorca persuaded me to accompany him to Granada, Spain, his native land. And a few days later I accepted with pleasure. I thought It would be good to see my parents once again,

When we arrived in Bordeaux, we heard the newsboys shouting abut the war in North Africa and the Spanish Revolution. In the headlines of practically all the newspapers were General Mola and Francisco Franco.

When we arrived in Irun, the Gendarmes and La Guardia Civil were inspecting passports from France to Spain and vice-versa.

I begged Lorca to return to Biarritz, France, and await the outcome of the movement, because I shall never forget the look that the Sergeant of La Guardia Civil gave Lorca when inspecting his passport.

After a few days in Biarritz, I could see Lorca was very nervous and was determined to go to Spain at any price.

That night I called my father who lives in Barcelona, long distance. He pleaded with me to remain where I was until the movement would calm.

Lorca was present and talked with my father for two minutes himself.

"Federico somehow my heart tells me not to go. I tell you I have a very strong presentiment not to go!"

"Oh well!" he replied, "What can they possibly do to us?"

"The Government, nothing! ... The Republicans are your friends and mine, ... but, "...(I answered)

"Yes?...Don't stop.! Say it, ... or perhaps you mean some of my poems, like "Romance de la Guardia Civil?" (He laughed.)

"Exactly, Federico!" I replied, "and I am glad you are coming to your senses! Let us wait a little longer. That won't last, ... I am sure it won't."

"Perhaps, ... Perhaps!" he murmured.

In the forenoon, the Spanish consul of Biarritz called the Hotel, and as Federico was in the shower, I answered.

The consul said that Lorca had a cable from Almeria, signed, Rafael Alberti, and he also informed me that my cousin Miguel Rabassa had been elected the Mayor of Barcelona,

Federico upon learning that his friend Rafael Alberti had been taken prisoner (according to the cable) looked at me, and exclaimed.

"Well paisano, I am leaving right now! Are you coming?"

"But Federico, I can not understand how can anyone send you or me any message when no one knows where we are, except my father?"

"Cierto! That's right, but someone must know!"

That evening Federico packed a small suitcase and left me in charge of his other belongings until he could advise me where to send them, and together we drove to the Spanish frontier and there we said Adios, the last Adios!

After having waited impatiently for over two weeks without a message, I decided to send Federico's trunk to his home at Fuente Vaqueros, Granada; and then across the Pyrenees to the Catalonian side.

When I arrived in Cervera, I crossed the frontier with a French passport, and I entered Spain. I felt that being on Catalonian soil would be much safer for me.

When the train stopped at Rosas, La Guardia Civil and several Italian officers inspected my passport and took me to La Commandancia. There I saw for the first time a picture of Conte Rossi.

They kept my passport and I was not to leave Rosas! And report every four hours day and night without fail; as they made it very clear to me that in case of not reporting I would be guilty of being a Marxist.

The Fascist applied the words Marxist and "Rojo" to the Republicans the Loyalists.

The penalty for such was DEATH!

It was in the city of Valencia that I learned of Lorca's tragedy.

For it was the sergeant of La Guardia Civil who revised our passports and reported Lorca. When El Teniente Medina de la Guardia Civil was informed he saw the opportunity for which he had waited since his and Lorca's childhood.

Many of the Spaniards believe that Lorca was murdered because of his poems against La Guardia Civil, but the real story is an entirely different one, ...

When Garcia Lorca was merely nineteen years of age, he was a student at the University of Granada where he met Salomerita la Gitana, a gypsy singer and dancer; perhaps the greatest we have ever had in Spain.

Lorca, being a writer of Folk Poetry, and as great as Calderon de la Barca and Lope de Vega, soon became popular among the Cante Hondo world, and Salomerita fell madly in love with him.

When Medina courted La Salomerita, it was without success and he was forced to abandon the idea, because it was the young and beautiful Salomerita who told Medina:

"Contigo no quiero na Miguelete!" (I want nothing to do with you, Civil Guard!)

But Medina never forgot, because La Guardia Civil never forgets, or forgives, because they are never wrong, because when they enter the civil guard force they become monsters and their joy is to kill the innocent!

And thus, when Medina learned of Garcia Lorca being at the French frontier, he forged the cable saying that Rafael Alberti was in prison. And when Lorca arrived in Spain, Medina was waiting for him in a private car with a forged warrant.

Lorca had been tricked!

And on a beautiful summer night Lorca saw Granada for the last time. Medina had his man and on a road close to Granada the following morning the corpse of Federico Garcia Lorca was discovered by two gypsies.

Spain and perhaps the entire world has lost a brilliant and honest man, and his literature, poems and folk-lore will live forever.

The swine, Medina mutilated Lorca's body, but his soul will live eternally!

How does Juan's story correlate with what historians say about Lorca's death? I consulted Ian Gibson's biography, *Federico Garcia Lorca, A Life*, which is, I believe, still considered the most authoritative work on Lorca's life.

At first it seemed to me that Juan's story and Gibson's writings on Lorca's last days couldn't be reconciled. Yet there was some validation to Juan's story in that this "Rafael Alberti" was known to be one of Lorca's best friends. Alberti at this time per historian Hugh Thomas in *The Spanish Civil War* was not in prison but safe in the Republican zone, and (as Gibson shows) Spaniards would brave death to rescue or help a friend. To a Spaniard, family came first, then friends, lastly the claims of government or politics. So Juan was right, Lorca had been tricked. The phony cable was the perfect bait to lure Lorca back to Spain.

Then I noticed a passage in Gibson's narrative where Lorca went to Madrid as the first rumblings of the developing Spanish Civil War were heard. Most of Lorca's friends told him not to go back to Andalusia but to stay in Madrid to be safe. Another of his friends there (a Falangist!) putting friendship before politics, told him the brutal truth that he would be safe only in France.

According to Gibson's chronology there was a period of three days or so associated with his Madrid trip in which his activities were not tacked down firmly. When Lorca was back in his native Granada and from then to his death, his day-to-day location and activities were well documented.

My belief is that Lorca, after the above conversation with his Falangist friend in Madrid, made a beeline to the airport and took a plane to Lyon where he hooked up with Juan. When he and Juan arrived back in Spain, in Irun, the Sergeant of La Guardia Civil (the Civil Guard) told his superiors about Lorca's presence on Spanish soil and maybe even heard Juan and Lorca talking about returning to France with a destination of Biarritz. If so, they could have easily guessed which hotel (or called them all with the bait of the phony cable). I think Lorca then flew direct to his home in Granada from Biarritz.

Was there a Sergeant or Lieutenant Medina, a personal villain? Possibly, but I doubt it. Was the story about Salomerita true? Possibly but I doubt that too. The Spanish understand about revenge and take seriously rivals in love, but I think they could not comprehend so easily the premeditated killing of Lorca who was considered practically a national asset, because he was simply deemed an Enemy of the State by some bureaucrat (such as the mayor of Granada). Instead they preferred to believe in a myth of the spurned rival in love.

Most of the help Lorca was given in his last days came from Falangists! Because Lorca was a good friend of their family they hid him—at risk of their own lives! And helped him to flee and hide out again. In the end when Lorca was caught they sought out Manuel de Falla, the composer who was a friend of Juan's. De Falla was a very modest conservative but non-political figure who was highly esteemed by all.

De Falla agreed to speak for Lorca, and while waiting to plead with the Mayor for his life he received the message that Lorca had been executed the night before at the "killing ground" outside of town where mass butchery routinely took place.

At this point in time Juan knew it was unsafe for him even with his French passport to reenter Spain so he came home to the Americas.

In the latter part of 1936, Juan composed the music, wrote the screenplay and directed the movie, "The Sea Devil," in English, and also the Spanish-speaking version (El Diablo Del Mar). The next photo shows a scene from the movie, a picture of Juan with acting crew, and snippets from the highly favorable movie review. If you can read the Spanish small print you will find the unbelievable. A leading man (Ramon Pereda) enthusiastically praising the director (Juan)!

In addition to "The Sea Devil," Juan also directed another movie, Corazones Que Esperan ("Hearts that Wait") for La Moderna Films.

Un grupo de actores que colaboraron al lado de Ramón Pereda, en la interesante película «El diablo del mar», dirigida y supervisada por Juan Duval, todos se interesan en leer la excelente revista española FILMS SELECTOS. Sentados: Víctor José Sabuni, corresponsal hispano y «doble» del maravilloso actor checoslovaco Francis Lederer, de la R K O-Radio Pictures; en el centro, el director Juan Duval y Ramón Pereda. Entre ellos se encuentran Barry Norton, El Chato, Daniel Rea, Gabriel Muñoz y el célebre (Drácula) Carlos Villarías.

Ramón Pereda y Mawita Castañeda en una escena de la interesante película «El diablo del mar», dirigida por Juan Duval.

trevistar al director de esta película. Es sorprendente la energía y preparación lor casi desconocido que ha contribuido definitiva al progreso de nuestra cinemat Pereda se expresó en términos elogioso —Nunca hubiera creído que era capaz una película con la seguridad y perfección lo ha hecho. Yo he sido dirigido por dire larga experiencia en la pantalla en inglés, nunca he quedado tan satisfecho del dire obra, y estoy seguro de que esta opinión comparten todos los que trabajaron en la Los que a menudo hablan de la producción ño! casi siempre desconocen las dificultad fuerzos que ella presupone. Juan Duval es e los mayores encomios no sólo por la fe y que ha desplegado, sino porque su obra, dob meritoria, es la obra de un hombre de ve experiencia. Cualquiera que lo hubiera visto d do las escenas de «El diablo del mar» no d de que estaba en presencia de un excelente preparado director.— Es de desear que el público comparta las del gran actor de habla hispana que, dada periencia cinemática que posee, tiene razones demás para discernir con acierto desde el pe de filmación la excelencia de una película.

Víctor José SAB

(Servicio exclusivo del «Sabuni International Syndicate».)

ifícil sintetizar en una página los múltiples detalles de la filmación de que es la primera producción de la compañía Theater Classic Pictures. erísticas son precisamente las que el público ha extrañado grandes estudios producidas en nuestra l una historia humana

Ramón Pereda y la encantadora artista Carmen Bally en una escena román tica de «El diablo del mar». (Fotos Servicio Ser

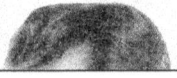

Clippings from *El Diablo Del Mar* ("The Sea Devil").

42

In 1937, Juan returned to Spain slipping "behind the lines" into Valencia, a Republican stronghold. There, and possibly in Madrid and Barcelona, he wrote poems and articles for the periodicals of the "liberation press." He was a strong supporter of the Spanish Republic (now fighting for its life) but he was neither anti-clerical, agnostic, atheistic, anti-religious or a communist. Though not a churchgoer, he always considered himself to be a Catholic. He believed in democracy and the separation of church and state.

Since the articles in the periodical *Solidarity* were probably written in Spanish, the following is Juan's translation of what he wrote for them:

ARTICLES PRINTED IN SPAIN IN 1937

*LA SOLIDARIDAD*

They came to you for arms,
munitions, and your moral support,
and you ignored them!

The Spanish prologue is ended,
but, the play still goes on.
Perhaps, you will have to play the part!

Oh! England and France,
How Could You?

In Mataro, one of Spain's greatest cities situated at the mouth of the Mediterranean Sea Coast, apparently from nowhere came Conte Rossi with an army of five thousand Fascists.

Immediately the men, women and children rushed to their Mayor demanding arms and munitions so they could defend the city.

But, at the Mayor's refusal the citizens of this great city defended themselves, with knives, stones, boiling water, and in every conceivable manner; because the Mayor had sold the arms of the people to Conte Rossi!

When "El Bandido de Calabria Rossi," received the password from the Mayor's spies with his fully equipped army, entered Mataro; and shooting and mutilating everything alive. It did not make any difference to the Fascists, they kill everything alive!

More than six thousand men, women, and children were massacred!

After the city completely surrendered, Conte Rossi, from the balcony of the City Hall, made a speech to his accomplices of crimes:

"Italy and Spain are sisters, with the same religion and ideas, the aggrandizement of our proud Latin race must not be contradicted by the Marxists, and the so called Democrats. We shall and will, exterminate everyone who would dare defy our Fascism, and if it becomes necessary we will destroy all fathers and mothers as well, because then and then only will we eliminate the seeds and their fruitification!

And now, I give you the beautiful Senoritas of our conquered city of Mataro. I hope my brave officers and soldiers, that you will do justice to their beauty, as well as to their very warm blood! Viva L'Italia! Viva, Viva!

Immediately in groups of no less than twelve, the Fascists hyenas went from house to house to fulfill the command of, "El Bastardo Conte Rossi!"

But raping and mutilating in the most vicious manner the innocent girls did not fulfill their beastly pleasures.

After killing the fathers and mothers of their victims, the fascists took what was left of the young girls from the ages of twelve to twenty-five, and at the next sunrise loaded them like sheep, approximately three thousand girls after having been raped and forced to the vilest villainy, were taken and forced to disrobe to the last garment, shaved their heads, and with revolvers in their hands, the brutal Fascists forced each girl to drink a pint of castor oil, and loading them in open trucks, paraded them through the streets.

Conte Rossi meanwhile was witnessing this vulgarity from the balcony of the City Hall with a few of his officers, the Bishop, and the Mayor, celebrating what he termed a great victory. He commanded the officers to give orders to the drivers of the trucks to drive much slower; so that he might have full benefit of the sight, and gaze upon the unfortunate girls in their agony.

As the fourth truck passed in front of the balcony, the Mayor shouted:

"Stop it! Stop it! Luisa! Mercedes! Excelencia señor Rossi, these two are my daughters... I demand their freedom, You have deceived me! Luisa, Mercedes!"

But Rossi with a slow smile took his automatic and discharged every bullet into Mayor's body. Rossi then ordered the Mayor's corpse removed, and exclaimed:

"Signor Mayor, you have violated my law! ... A Fascist never deceives!"

The people of Mataro shall never forget this tragic event, and the criminal monster Conte Rossi..Never! Never!


Hugh Thomas' *The Spanish Civil War* is, I believe, still considered the most definitive account of that horrible war. In it he mentions a Conte Rossi (Arconovaldo Bonaccorsi), "a fanatical fascist with a red beard" who arrived to help the Nationalists on Majorca repel a Republican Catalan expeditionary force. The Catalans fled back to the mainland and "Thereafter, Majorca remained for some months the private fief of the 'Conte Rossi'...It was now that the murders of working-class Majorcans reached their height."

The detailed account given above by Juan of Conte Rossi's attack on the city of Mataro appears to constitute new historical information that was unavailable to Thomas, since his book index shows no entry for "Mataro" and no further information on Conte Rossi's activities! It sounds like the killing in Majorca was merely a "warm-up" to what Rossi did in Mataro. Mataro is part of Catalonia and located on the coast a short distance northeast of Barcelona.

Historian Michael Alpert in *A New International History of the Spanish War*, writing much later than Thomas, gives similar colorful details about Conte Rossi's tenure on Mallorca ending with new information regarding his recall by Italy from Mallorca in January, 1937 at the urging of the British government. However no further mention of him is made (nor is there any reference to "Mataro" in his index).

The latest popular history of the Spanish Civil War, *The Battle for Spain: The Spanish Civil War 1936–1939* by Anthony Beevor, offers even less detailed information on Conte Rossi. Ironically, it is the Wikipedia that yielded my next clue.

The Wikipedia reference on *Arconovaldo Bonaccorsi* yields the further useful information that Conte Rossi was remanded to Rome for several months, then returned to Spain to help subdue Malaga and Catalonia, for which he was awarded two commendations by Italian generals. This timetable could allow the alleged "Mataro Massacre" to be dated to May-July of 1937.

In short, the historical record (available to me) places Conte Rossi near Mataro around this time and Juan, likely nearby in Barcelona where he could have talked to survivors. Conceivably there are bloody details of Rossi's subduing of Catalonia in Italian historical records (but not likely Spanish).

There is a truism about war; that the winning side writes the history books afterwards. For any scholars out there interested in hearing the other side, here is something of interest for them. Mataro may still have a few old folk, or their descendents, that can validate the above account.

From the internal evidence of the account, it is obvious Juan was not there in Mataro as a direct eyewitness to the events. What he must have done was to listen to oral accounts of survivors, and as a writer, put them into chronological and dramatic order. And his presence in Barcelona at this time, which is about 30 miles from Mataro, would be understandable. His family still lived in Barcelona and it is highly likely he would have visited them after leaving Valencia (where he wrote a poem dated July, 1937).

Other excerpts from Juan's writings:

> When the famous government of Burgos ordered the new stamped money, the Commandante of Mallorca like every city under the domination of Franco's regime, took great advantage of the Spanish middle class, and what is known as the blue-bloods.
>
> The severe order was proclaimed, and the people were told that the paper money had to be stamped by the new system, otherwise it would lose it's full value.
>
> Immediately people started going to the banks to have their notes stamped, ignorant of the outcome.
>
> When a citizen would go into a bank and present for instance, the amount of five thousand pesetas, the military officer in charge stamped every note with, "Arriba Espana" Up Spain!
>
> But the depositor received a receipt for the five thousand pesetas and was told to return in about a week.
>
> When the depositor called for the money, instead of the bank paying the full amount, they would pay only two thousand five hundred pesetas, one half only, and the depositor was forced to sign a receipt, and were given the following: "We have received from Mr. and Mrs. _____, the amount of 2,500 pesetas a donation for the great cause, and the Salvation of Spain."
>
> In every city under Franco's regime, the Fascist propagandists exposed the Loyalists to the lowest infamy.
>
> According to the Fascists in Valencia, Barcelona, Zaragoza, Alicante, Oviedo, Santander, Salamanca, and Bilbao, the Loyalists were burning the Convents and Churches, and were killing everything religious and sacred.

But, what the Fascists did not tell or print was the fact that in Barcelona in particular, the majority of the Churches, Convents and Monasteries were not only accomplices of Franco, but fortifications, fighting, and killing the Loyalists, which Franco called his fifth column.

In contrast to this when I debarked at La Linea de la Concepcion across from Gibraltar, I learned through an old friend of mine that Father Anton was still teaching and was in excellent health.

I was delighted because in my whole life I have never seen a man as close to the great philosophy of Christ.

Padre Anton was a priest and a preacher whose sole mission in life was to serve God, and to teach unfortunate children whose parents were unable to pay the city and state for even primary schooling.

When with many difficulties Padre Anton had built a small institution with approximately six hundred children under his care, the private, city and state schools, monasteries and convents soon complained bitterly of Father Anton's activities with a false accusation of insanity and of being a Communist, to the Bishop of Barcelona.

The Bishop assisted by the state and with a document signed by the Pope, suspended and expelled Father Anton from all rights of the Church, and also from receiving the small pittance he earned at Sunday mass.

In the beginning of August in the year 1936, Father Anton was established in Valencia teaching there the under-privileged children. His old age and poor health coupled with the miseries the state and Bishop caused him, forced the good Padre to take to his bed.

Then when the Fascists entered Valencia, like Federico Garcia Lorca, Padre Anton was executed.

The voice that commanded, "Fire" was a Rector's, a clergyman and he was the officer of the firing squad!

I wrote and pleaded with the English consul to aid the Loyalists through his government, but all was in vain.

On the first cargo boat via Marseilles, I booked passage, but not before being tortured with "La Cuerda de los Presos."

It felt good to be on a French boat.'

On my arrival in Marseilles I straightway visited the Spanish, American and English consulates, begging for assistance, for arms, munitions and food for the poor defenseless Spaniards who were seeking refuge on the French frontier, but again and again all my efforts were in vain.

The French government instead of aiding the Spaniards who wanted to fight to preserve liberty and freedom, not the French people, but the government, placed the Spaniards under a "Martial Law," and in concentration camps.

England and France ignored the fact that the war of Spain was a prologue to their drama, and a tragic epilogue to the rest of the Democracies!

Mexico's government and it's people helped the Loyalists, morally and materially, and moreover opening their frontiers to the children of war, offering shelter, food and moral support.

People of Mexico, I salute you!


And, when at last as night falls, a vessel is pulling up anchor, it's destination America, ... North America!

As we are sailing under the cloudy skies I realize that I am leaving, perhaps forever, the historical Mediterranean Sea, and La Cordillera (chain of mountains) along the coast, now in shadow.

Even the old vessel seemed to feel my nostalgia, which moving slowly pays her respects with me to the brave peoples of Spain, still fighting against brutality, to defend their freedom, ... their peace, ... their democracy.

The sea is calm, very calm, and as the wind softly caresses the gentle waves I glance into the water to see reflected a melancholy moon, which rhythmically and very clearly projects into my mind, ...scenes of the past.

The happy crowds in a Plaza de Toros watching a Corrida, then a Fronton, a Soccer game, The Ferias, Romerias, ... Verbenas, Meriendas de Campo, La Fiesta Mayor, ...

Then, the strange life of the gypsies in the famous Albaicin of Granada, night after night singing and playing their guitars, while the daughters of King Pharaoh, fascinated by the oddity of the cry of their native barbarian music, and are gracefully moving their beautiful curves to a passionate crescendo, till they cry for their Prince; "Come my lover!... Take me, ... brutally, beautifully, sublimely!"

We have passed Barcelona, Valencia, Almeria, and as the vessel points North we enter the Atlantic Ocean. The waves of the Mediterranean curling desperately are rising in all their might to reach our stern and the stars displayed by the American flag.

A pathetic sound from the turbulent and desolate waves left behind us rings in my ears the familiar cry!

"Wait, ... please wait for me!"

Like the Spanish refugees I heard in Cervera, France. Three thousand of them begging the French Government, pleading with the identical cry:

"We want arms! We want peace! We want Liberty! We want to kill Franco! Please, no put us in concentration Camp! No! No! No!"

Still so disturbed by the smell of blood that I could hardly think, but the sound of a bell announcing breakfast, made me turn to the young steward, who with a pleasant smile walked away understandingly.

The sky is still dark with dreary clouds that we slowly leave behind us; like a long procession, and as I turn the last page of the forgotten, the vision of the great immortals surge before me, I see them in black, mourning for the destruction of that which they so valiantly built. The Spain of Cid Campeador, Cervantes, Guzman el Bueno, Goya, Prim, Mendez Pelayo, Baroja, Perez de Ayala, Sol y Ortega, Christobal Colon, Padre Anton, Federico Garcia Lorca, and thousands of others, great men whose sacrifices for human happiness and freedom to bring Liberty, Love and Peace to all mankind was their doctrine, their faith, their philosophy.

To-day in the twentieth-century in a world of so called progress and civilization, again great and good honest men, innocent women, and defenseless children are being murdered, mutilated, raped and tortured by Franco . . . by the Moors, by Nazism, and Fascism. What Price Power, "WHAT PRICE POWER!"

Oh! England and France how could you wash your hands of the injustice done to the Spanish people who fought to the last man against the brutality of the Dictators.

Juan's voice of anguish expressed in the previous pages over the terrible Civil War happenings he witnessed was one of many voices. Carlos Bauer in his book, *Cries From a Wounded Madrid, Poetry of the Spanish Civil War*, used a quote from Albert Camus which captures well the outraged feelings of many people at that time. "It was in Spain that men learned that one can be right and still be beaten, that force can vanquish spirit... It is this without doubt, which explains why so many men throughout the world regard the Spanish drama as a personal tragedy."

There is in Spain today, it is said, a sincere interest in finding out the truth about that most awful war.

An unusual variant of that same interest in revisiting the past is the doings of a group of forensic archaeologists as reported in *Archaeology* magazine a few years ago. This group assisted some rural Spanish villagers to identify the remains of their deceased relatives. Mass unmarked graves were common in the Spanish Civil War. These archaeologists were able to identify some specific individuals (using genetic markers of living relatives) who were "repatriated" to family burial plots.

Only a few miscellaneous writings of Juan remain (and are being presented here). I never saw any of Juan's early poetry books. Without titles or other publication data they would be impossible to find. What remains of his poetry on the Spanish Civil War is presented here below with individual description or commentary.

Of poems, his *Pa Quien Tocan Las Campanas* ("For Whom the Bells Toll") is quite interesting, probably his most sophisticated and certainly the most impassioned. Here is a translated excerpt showing some of its dramatic fire:

Look how much we love you
Brave Land of Spain
That we give you our blood
So that you may drink, that you might live.

This poem is dated "July, 1937, Valencia, Spain," which confirms Juan was behind the Republican lines for a time.

In constructing this poem Juan used a phrase of John Donne's (from the famous "No Man is an Island" Meditation xvii of his *Devotions*) as the structural theme and refrain of his poem written in July, 1937. Ernest Hemingway used the same identical phrase for the title of his famous novel about the Spanish Civil War *For Whom the Bell Tolls*, published October 21, 1940.

It was likely just coincidence that two authors would use the same source, except that Hemingway was in Spain in 1937 representing the North American Newspaper Alliance. It's conjecture of course, but he could have seen Juan's poem in one of the local periodicals and thought what a great dramatic impact using the Donne quote, which elsewhere includes, "any man's death diminishes me," could give to any writing on the Spanish Civil War.

## PA QUIEN TOCAN LAS CAMPANAS

Ván las doce de la noche
Canta el Viejo vigilante,
Y el campanario las dobla
con el grito de venganza.

Que viénen los moros gritan!
Los serranos de Linares
Que viénen los moros gritan!
Todos los Pueblos de España.

Entran los moros bastardos
Violando a las mozuelas
Asesinando a las madres
Porque a sus hijas defienden.

Descansan bajo la tierra
los cementerios de España,
Seis-millones de inocentes
Que los moros mutilaron.
España si serás grande
Que tus hijos por ti muéren,
Pá quién tocan las campanas
Pá quién di, pá quién!

Mas no te olvides del canto
De "Abajo La Tirania"
Pá que el fruto venidero
Al traidor le haga Justicia.
El Prólogo ha terminado
Mas la Comedia prosigue,

A Dios que ha sido testigo
Le dejamos nuestra causa,
A Dios bueno y justiciero
Justicia al traidor gritamos!

Pá quién tocan las campanas
Que lloran sin compasión,
Pá quién tocan pá quién tocan
Pá quién ésta vez pá quién.
El pueblo húye a los montes
Atacando a los infames,
Con sus machetes sangrientes
Que han clavado a los cobardes.
Todo el pueblo de Aragon
Se defiénde mana a mano,
Contra el traidor español
Y los moros que ha comprado.
Pá quién tocan las campanas!
Pá quién ésta véz pá quién!

Madrid, Andalucia y Valencia,
Bañan de sangre las calles
Del pueblo qué pecho a pecho
Contra los moros se baten.
Madres, hijas, hijos, padres
Ancianos y los de téta,
Con el cuchillo en la mano,
Todos, todos se defiénden!
Pá quién tocan las campanas,
Pá quién ésta vez pá quién!

Sécas sediéntas tus huertas
Sin la siéga se han quedado,
Por no dar agua tus Norias
Tus Molinos ya han cesado.
Mira cuánto te querremos
Tierra de España bravia,
Qué te damos nuestra sangre
Pá que bebas, pá que vivas.

Las campanas ya han callado
Mas el Éco que no ha muerto,
Corre a tras de los infames
Redoblando a sus conciencias,

Desde el marmol de las tumbas
Oiremos gemir el llanto,
Del traidor que infamemente
Quiso robar nuestra España.

Abajo la tirania, abajo!
viva el pueblo proletario!

Mientras las campanas doblan
El grito que libra España,
Llega una vóz misteriosa
Y repica el campanario.

Pá quién tocan las campanas,
Pá quién esta vez pá quién?
Pá el traidor de nuestra España!

Por Juan Duval
Julio – 1937. Valencia España.

# FOR WHOM THE BELLS TOLL

It's 12:00 o'clock midnight
Sings the night watchman
And the belltower tolls
With the cry of vengeance

The moors are coming cry
The mountaineers of Linares!
The moors are coming cry
All the towns of Spain!

Enter the bastard moors
Violating the young girls
Assassinating the mothers
Because they defend their daughters

Resting below ground
In the cemeteries of Spain
Six million innocents
Who the moors mutilated.
Spain, you shall become great
Because your children die for you
For whom do the bells toll
For whom, tell me. For whom!

Never forget the chant
Of "Down with Tyranny"
So that our posterity
To the traitor will give Justice
The Prologue has finished
Now the Comedy proceeds

To God, who has been witness
We leave our cause
To God, good and just,
Justice for the traitor we shout!

For whom do the bells toll?
Who cry without compassion.
For whom toll, for whom toll
For whom this time, for whom?

The townspeople escape to the mountains
Attacking the infamous ones
With their bloody machetes
That have slashed at the cowards
All the towns of Aragon
Defend themselves hand to hand
Against the Spanish traitor
And the moors they have bought
For whom do the bells toll?
For whom this time, for whom!

Madrid, Andalusia and Valencia,
Wash the streets with blood
Of the townspeople who breast to breast
Batter against the moors
Mothers, daughters, sons, fathers

Old ones and those suckling at the breast,
With the knife in their hand
All, all defend themselves!
For whom do the bells toll,
For whom this time, for whom!

Dry and thirsty your orchards
Without the harvest they remain
For not giving water to your Pumps,
Your Windmills now have stopped.
See how much we love you
Brave land of Spain
That we give you our blood
For you to drink, so that you may live

The bells now are silent
Just the Echo which has not died,
Runs behind the infamous ones
Redoubling strength against their consciences.

From the marble of the tombstones
We will hear moaning the chant
Against the traitor who infamously
Sought to steal our Spain.

Down with Tyranny, down!
Long live the people
While the bells toll
The cry that liberates Spain,
Arrives a mysterious voice
And the bell tower resounds

For whom do the bells toll
For whom this time, for whom?
For the Traitor of our Spain!

By Juan Duval
July-1937. Valencia, Spain

Juan used the bell imagery in the reverse way Donne used it. In the Donne meditation the ringing of bells celebrates human life; in Juan's poem the bells toll as a dirge (as they often did bringing bad news of battles and calamities to the towns of Europe over the centuries).

Toward the end of the poem the bells become silent, then "arrives a mysterious voice" and the bells intensify their tolling again. I think this "mysterious voice" is the "judgment of posterity giving Justice to the Traitor." Juan had faith in Spain's future; that it would eventually repudiate fascism and dictatorship and achieve representative government. But he knew enough of war to perceive that the Republican Army was already slipping towards eventual defeat despite its many brave battles.

All the Spanish Civil War poetry I have read is "concrete," impassioned and immediate. The farsightedness of Juan's poem is a testimony to his historical and social vision, transcending the immediate and the impassioned. This "prophetic vision" pops up occasionally in Spanish history. A good example is the unknown writer, living in an Arab Spain in the year 800 A.D., who wrote about a future Spain that would be Christian. It took nearly 700 years to happen but Ferdinand and Isabella brought it about. Juan's vision came to be within half a century! I think his poem exceptional—and perhaps unique—and hope that Spanish poetry experts will give it a reading.

Juan "prophetic insight" was accurate in another matter. On the title page to the *La Solidaridad* writings (referenced earlier) he uses figurative language to warn England and France that failure to help in the "prologue" (the Spanish Civil War) makes it likely they will have to "play the part" (fight Fascist Germany and Italy) later. That prophecy came true only too soon!

"For Whom the Bells Toll" and other Civil War themed poems of Juan's were likely published in *La Solidaridad* along with his prose articles. There was a massive outpouring of Spanish poetry in the first two years of the war, even on the Nationalist side. This intriguing insight and many others come from Carlos Bauer's book mentioned earlier.

Bauer explains that not only did Spain's recognized poets turn out impassioned war poetry, anyone and everyone was encouraged to do so. The volume was staggering. Much of it was printed in two major periodicals, *Hora de España* ("Spain's Hour") and *El Mono Azul* ("The Blue Overall"). He says there were many other periodicals as well. Juan's *La Solidaridad* ("Solidarity") must have been one of them.

Bauer mentions two literary giants, Lorca and Machado, whose works sharpened the interest in Spanish poetry in the years before the war. Of these two, Lorca was a friend of Juan's and Antonio Machado had publicly praised Juan's earlier poems. So Juan did have some reputation as a poet before the war.

Bauer describes an early anthology of Civil War poetry, *Poetas En La España Leal*, published in July, 1937, to commemorate the Second International Congress of Anti-Fascist Writers, held that year in Valencia, Barcelona, and Madrid. Among the participants were Malcolm Cowley, W.H. Auden, Stephen Spender, Pablo Neruda, Cesar Vallejo, Octavio Paz, Andre Malraux and Tristan Tzara. Published by the government publishing house, *Ediciones Españolas*, under the direction of the editors of *Hora De España*, this anthology brought together forty-four poems, almost all of which had previously appeared in *Hora De España*.

So, Juan was there in Valencia the very same month that international writer's conference was going on. It's very possible he attended some of it; maybe he even contributed one of his poems. A long shot perhaps, but a review of that work's index might be worthwhile. If not available on the Internet, it may be through the *Biblioteca Nacional* in Madrid.

The brief poems *Con Su Mirada a Granada* and *Soneto* are paeans to his friend Garcia Lorca. The title of the first means, "With His Glance Toward Granada."

## CON SU MIRADA A GRANADA

Con su Mirada a Granada
El álto quién vive diéron!
Noche triste! Triste noche!
Granada, Granada mia!
Vengo a Éspana porqué es mia!
soy español de Granada!
Mi crimen sóy un Poeta,
Garcia Lorca me llaman.

Yó Medina dóy el mando!
eres mi preso Gitano!

Y en podér de aquél hereje,
cayó el posta mas gránde
el escritór mas castizo,
y el español más honrrado.
Con altanera su frente,
y su pecho palpitante;
cayó inérte nuestro Lorca,
con su mirada a Granada.

## SONETO

Granada tu Granada estaba triste;
La Luz del Sol, al firmamento apagaba,
Mas cuándo ya resignada, a la eternal obscuridad
se oyó de los altos Cielos, tu grito de viva Espana.
Hóy que las Almas, en tu memoria vivan;
Cual masas lloran tu inevitable ausencia,
Tu "Romancero Gitano" Tus Poemas en fin todo;
Ya llegáron por la brisa a nuestras Almas.
El Sol, volvió ha renacer, las nubes cediéron paso!
y todas aquellas Almas que tu vóz iluminó,
Al compás de un Fandanguillo, con su Trabuco en la mano
como fieras, Una a Una hasta la muerte lucharon.
Las guitarras ya no lloran, los Gitanos ya no Cantan.
El Albaicin vive en lúto, los trabucos ya han callado.
Mas los herejes que quédan, al poder de nuestra España
se rendirán ante el arte, ante Tú Lorca el Gitano.
El Alma de España, por el espacio perdida vá!
El Albaicin, Andalucia y Granada,
Sin ti, quedó triste y desolada,
y désde entónces, querido!
SANGRE SANGRERA HA SANGRADO.

—Por Juan Duval

This next poem, *La Argentinita*, is a paean to Juan's friend and dance partner, Antonia Merce.

## LA ARGENTINITA

Encarnació que encarnas toda una Espana
menudita de vivéz y enorme encanto,
Qúe has sabido conquistar extrañas tierras
Embelleciendo tódo el Arte del Levante.

Ya lléga la Argentinita
la embajadora del arte
Anda jaleo jaleo,
y alimentar la nostalgia.
Que noche, que hermosa éres!
Que expectáculo más grande
todo me parece un sueño
lleno de bellezas gratas.

Cierrénse todas las puertas
las lúces yá medio apagan
se enciénden las candilejas
El público inquiéto aplaude.
Yá el telón sube altanero
Yá en el foro se abre paso,
Al compás de un Fanfandanguillo
La Argentinita bailando.

Y entre Bravos, Grito y Palmas!
del público entusiasmado,
La Argentinita bailo!
El Albaicin, Toda la Sierpe y Triana.

Como Vega, Calderon y el Genial Lorca "El Gitano"
Vivirás eternamente, en el fondo de mi Alma.
Menudita de vivéz y enorme encanto
Encarnación que encarnas tóda una España.
                    —Por Juan Duval

La Argentinita, ("the lady from Argentina") was a nickname for Antonia Merce. C.S. Forester wryly notes in his historical novel, *The Gun*, "The Spanish habit of conferring nicknames on any one of note, from kings to bullfighters."

The use of name diminutives such as the extra "it" in Merce's nickname in the poem title is also typical Spanish usage for close friends. The same tendency may be even more pronounced in Russian. As a noted translator, Princess Alexandra Kropotkin, of *War and Peace* comments, "Russian families... use so many diminutives of given names...are particularly confusing to a foreign reader...."

Tacked into one line of this poem, Juan uses Lorca's nickname of *El Gitano* ("The Gypsy") to help enshrine him alongside literary greats Lope de Vega and Calderon.

I had my own experience with a Spanish diminutive. Juan used to call me "Joselito." "Jose" is of course "Joseph" in Spanish. The "ito" made it an affectionate diminutive. There is further humor in the fact that one of the greatest bullfighters of that time was also called "Joselito."

The last poem—my favorite—is not a Civil War poem. It's titled *La Humanidad Es Asi* ("Humanity is Like That"). Deceptively simple in structure and wording yet deeply incisive, it tells something of the poet's philosophy of life. I think Juan might have been influenced by E.E. Cummings when he wrote this one. Judge for yourself.

### LA HUMANIDAD ES ASI

Mercaderes ván y viénen,
Del Mercado del amor.
De comprar un pedazito,
De carne de su sabór.

En las Selvas de Pasion
Las Fieras viénen y ván.
En busca del bocadito,
Dando muerte a su rival.

El buen labrador cultiva,
El fruto que dá la tierra.
Más cuando ya está maduro
Se lo roban y lo venden.

Cómo, en la Tierra y Mar,
El grande se cóme el chico.
Sea Caza, Robo, o Compra,
Viénen y van Mercaderes,
En busca del Bocadito.

Yo vívo, de Sol a Sol
Y de náda más entiendo
En dios confio el destino
y no en los sabios del pueblo.

Los únos quiéren mandar!
Los otros enriquecér,
Algúnos quiéren matar!
Y nadie favorecer.

Es la Santa Humanidad
Un misterio para mi:
Que poco me ha de importar,
La Humanidad es asi!

## HUMANITY IS LIKE THAT

Merchants go and come
From the marketplace of love
To buy a little piece
Of meat of that flavor

In the Jungles of Passion
The Furies come and go
In search of a little mouthful
Giving death to their rival

The good laborer cultivates
The fruit which the land gives
But then when it's ripe
They steal it from him and sell it

As on the Land and in the Sea
The big one eats the little one
Whether it's Catch Steal or Buy
Come and go the Merchants
In search of the Little Bite

I live, from Sun to Sun
And of nothing else I understand
In god confide my destiny
And not in the wise men of the town

Some of them want to send!
Others want to enrich themselves
Some want to kill!
And no one wants to do you well

This is Holy Humanity
A mystery for me
How little it should matter to me
Humanity is like that!

# 4

# Hollywood, 1937–1954

In 1941 the big Hollywood movie, "Blood and Sand" came out, with star-power galore including Tyrone Power, Linda Darnell, Rita Hayworth, and Anthony Quinn. Leonard Maltin, the film critic, in his *Movie Guide*, 2007 Edition, called it a "pastel remake of Valentino's (1922) silent film...." Juan had lots to say about it as you can see from this "Letters to the Editor" clipping from the *Hollywood Citizen News*. This article shows Juan in a scholarly mode:

"Blood and Sand"

Town Meeting: No wonder South America, Mexico, Central America, and Spain protest against the Hollywood films which treat of Hispanic life. One would think that the director of "Blood and Sand" would have surrounded himself with people who were familiar technically and psychologically with this immortal work of Blasco Ibanez. Had anyone with any "say" about the production known better, the serenade to Carmen would have been a dignified romantic love scene, as befitting the great matador, Juan Gallardo, instead of a cheap burlesque.

Again, during the final bull-fight, the orchestra played "Jarabe Tapatio," a Mexican regional dance, and with all due respect to the Mexican people, I am certain they will agree with me how inappropriate this song is in such a typical Spanish scene. The song supposedly sung by Dona Sol in honor of Juan Gallardo, is not only ridiculous but an insult to the Cante Hondo, the traditional Deep Songs of Spain. The Sevillanas dance, the bull-fight dance, and the dance by Dona Sol and Manolo in the Café are corruptions of their original Iberian character.

All in all, music, costumes, technical supervision, screenplay and direction indicate very little respect and knowledge of Spanish life and fall far short of catching the essence of the immortal work of Don Vicente Blasco Ibanez' "Blood and Sand."

—JUAN DUVAL

Blasco Ibañez died in 1928 so he was not around to complain about what the movie makers did to his novel. But Juan did it for him. I'm not sure if Juan and Blasco Ibañez were personally acquainted but Ibañez knew of Juan's earlier works and publicly praised them.

Juan in North Africa in 1942 with the U.S. Army Air Corps, possibly near Tunis where Juan was sent in 1916 when he was in the French Foreign Legion.

**Juan in Air Force uniform, North Africa, 1942.**

He never spoke of this campaign. I believe he must have been used in the communication/intelligence sector. He fluently spoke French, Spanish, and Italian, and soldiers speaking these languages were allied with the Germans and would have been prisoners when successful Allied operations began in North Africa (such as in Morocco and Tunisia). This, I recall, is where Patton spanked Rommel!

As a U.S. soldier Juan had fought in two World Wars and been a soldier in North Africa in both these wars. Juan was an immigrant whose "path to citizenship" was more rigorous than any being proposed today.

He once told me about the horrors of trench warfare in France in World War I, the countless horrifying charges back and forth in No-Man's Land, the ceaseless artillery barrages, and the mud. He aimed where they told him and shot when they said to. It was massive and impersonal. In all this time there was only once when he thinks he might have killed one German soldier but wasn't really sure. Nor was he proud of it. Like millions of citizen-soldiers he did what was required of him without complaint.

Later in 1942 he went to Radio School in Madison, Wisconsin but was honorably discharged from the U.S. Army Air Corps (Truax Field), the next year for health reasons; with a glowing letter of recommendation dated February 11, 1943, from his commanding officer, Commander W.T. Bruxton, Jr.

```
                 627th TECHNICAL SCHOOL SQUADRON
                 ARMY AIR FORCE TECHNICAL SCHOOL
                 Truax Field, Madison, Wisconsin              WTB/pwl


                                              February 11, 1943


     TO WHOM IT MAY CONCERN:

          This is to certify that Juan Bellavista has been a student
     at Radio School at Truax Field for approximately two months  and has
     been attached to Technical School Squadron 627, of which I am Commander.
     He is being  released from the  Military Service of the United States
     by reason of ill health.

          He is inteligent and is well informed on world affairs.  He is
     a writer and speaks Spanish, Italian, French, Portuguese and English
     fluently.

          While in this Squadron his conduct has been excellent and his
     efficience as a soldier has been excellent.  It gives me great
     pleasure to recommend him to any one who may be concerned.


                                         W.  T.  BRUTON JR.,
                                         Captain, Air Corps,
                                         Commanding.
```

Juan's Air Force Letter of Reference.

The caption on this 1944 family photo is in Juan's own writing, "my mother, father, sister, and friends."

In 1944 he went to Mexico and wrote two screenplays for Santander Productions, *Los Piratas* ("The Pirates"), and *Camino Real* ("The King's Highway").

In 1945 Juan directed *Gardel No Ha Muerto* for *Film Mundiales de la Argentina* on location in Cuba. In an interview with Antonio Villazon prior to that shooting, Juan said, "Like a good Latin, the movie spoken in Spanish has always interested me." ("*Como buen Latino, siempre me ha interesado el cine hablado en Espanol.*")

# Una Entrevista con el Director Juan Duval

**HA VENIDO A DIRIGIR «GARDEL NO HA MUERTO» ES CIUDADANO NORTEAMERICANO. COMENZO SU CARRERA EN HOLLYWOOD EN 1929. CONSIDERA A CUBA EXCELENTE LUGAR PARA LAS FILMACIONES. POR ANTONIO VILLAZON**

(Por Antonio VILLAZON)

Cuban newspaper article entitled "An Interview with the Director Juan Duval" while he was in Cuba directing *Gardel No Ha Muerto.*

Juan, about 1945.

Juan in 1946 with Tyrone Power in "The Razor's Edge."

Around December of 1947 my mother, then Carmen Bonelli, entered Juan's life. As I learned later it was love at first sight for both of them and many lives were drastically changed by this meeting. My mother had lots of Spanish relatives in San Francisco (including my great uncle Nick who was Basque) so she must have met Juan for one of their parties or through the Union Española. Cultural ties have been historically strong among most immigrant groups.

A month or two later I was on my way south and was placed in the Los Angeles Orphanage on Vine Street below Sunset. I was told my mother was not well and couldn't care for me for a while. Thus I arrived in Hollywood from San Francisco's Chinatown (my great Aunt Tia Carmen spoke Spanish with a Chinese accent). At my new home I may have even slept in Marilyn Monroe's bed! I was told she had been a prior resident of this facility. I was to spend nearly two years there.

Love, and the choices people make with it, is not always easy and comfortable. For my mother to love Juan above all else, she had to go against much of her Spanish culture, particularly her Catholicism. I doubt that divorce was even legal in Spain at the time. She also had to deal with her guilt for leaving my father, who like myself, was a blameless victim in this small personal drama.

Juan saw that my mother got psychiatric help to work things out but with his Freudian-tipped questions about her feelings for her mother and father, she quickly dumped him.

Meanwhile, I got along fine at the "Home" and walked over to Vine Street School every day with my dorm group. Many of my playmates were true orphans. Others like me had parents in "Crisis."

As time went on, my outside visits away from the home increased and I spent some weekends at their apartment and was treated to pony rides, Sheriff's rodeos, trips to Griffith Park Zoo, picnics, trips to the ocean, and other marvelous entertainments.

**Myself and Juan at sheriff's rodeo in August of 1949.**

Juan encouraged me to play "Let's Pretend" games, even giving me mustaches to play detective.

In 1948 Juan was technical adviser to Charles Vidor for the bullfight scenes in "The Loves of Carmen," as well as a background extra.

On June 18, 1949 Juan and my mother were married in a civil ceremony during the period I was still in the orphanage. In the divorce from my father the judge awarded my mother fifty dollars per month child support but she asked him to lower it to thirty-five. She was working as a clerk at this time and Juan was picking up small movie parts. Although I never saw their marriage certificate I know they were married because she received a veteran's widow pension after his death.

Juan with me the following month on the grounds of the Home, where I had broken my wrist hunting grasshoppers.

Saturday and Sunday were visiting days and days for family trips. Going to the beach was my favorite.

In the first of these beach photos Juan shows his sense of humor with the annotation, "To heck with holding these poses, where's the latrine?"

How many kids are lucky enough to live so close to the Pacific Ocean? And to have a stepfather who cares?

Juan never once said a single derogatory thing about my biological father. My father was orphaned by the 1906 earthquake and never got past the fourth grade. When I was a baby and had colic he would rock me until I fell asleep when my mother couldn't. He took me to movies when I was five and did all he knew to be a good father. Nor did my mother ever utter a disrespectful comment about him. Juan treated me as if I were his own son.

When I was older I thought about all of this, concluding he had been a model stepfather. Simply because children need all the loving parenting and guidance they can get, from all parents, stepparents, grandparents, or significant others. Especially if the parent figures in their life don't compete with each other and always put the child first. I was lucky that way with my stepfather and father, but not my wicked (ignorant) stepmother who viewed me as a competitor. Nor was I lucky with grandparents as I had none; they were dead or scattered to the four winds. And kids today who have them, pay them no mind, not knowing the "nuclear" family is historically a recent experiment while extended families had been the norm through most of human history. Paying more attention to an Electronic Guru (the Internet) instead of knowing and caring adults, they struggle to learn how to be human.

In 1949 Juan co-authored with Victor Granados the musical score for "Daughter of the West," and had a small part in that movie as well.

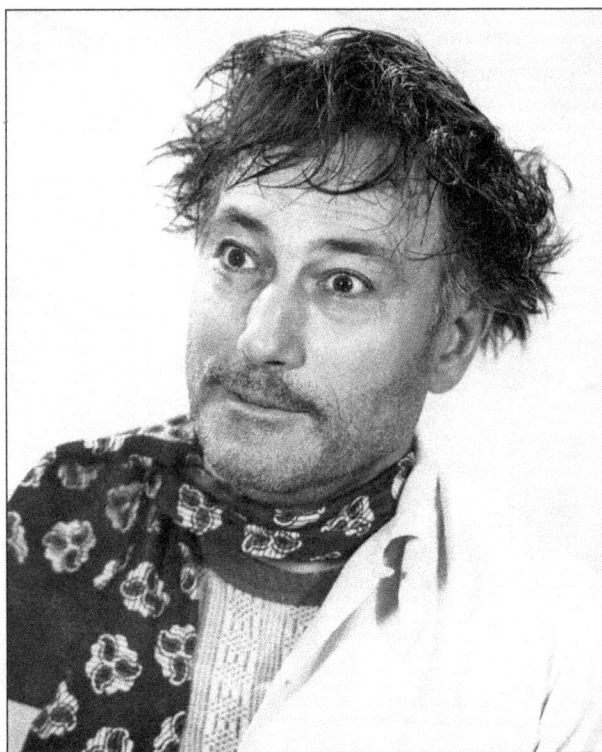

In 1950 Juan was in "Crisis" with Cary Grant and Paula Raymond.

When I left the orphanage early in 1950 this is the first apartment the three of us lived. It was 1238½ N. Harper in Hollywood, a few blocks from the Sunset Strip, and a nightclub where years later I saw a beginning rock group, The Doors, playing their first gig on the Strip.

My mother and I in front of our first apartment.

Our next door neighbor, who was a friend of Juan's, had a small house that bordered our apartment building on the east side. He was Warner Anderson, star of 1950s' "Destination Moon." A friendly neighbor and gentleman.

In February of 1950 we visited the home of a friend of Juan's, the novelist Alyce Pollock, author of *Don Gaucho*, the story of a Spanish-Argentine aristocrat who in the 19th century led the gauchos (cowboys) of Argentina in a bid for freedom from the Spanish crown. Thematically, the book was about struggle for political liberation and freedom. The same theme that engaged Juan personally in Valencia in 1937, when he tried as a writer to help defend the Spanish Republic that Generalissimo Franco hijacked.

Some time this same year (1950) Juan attended a party at the home of a friend, John McIntyre, an actor who had done well with cowboy "Wagon Master" roles. Also at the party was Emilio Osta, also a friend of Juan's, and a talented concert pianist, and specialist in interpreting Spanish/Latin American music. The host brought out a tape recorder and Emilio, without advance study, played Juan's newest composition, a lengthy ballet entitled *El Zapaterito* ("The Little Cobbler") straight through. Emilio and his lovely sister Teresita (a talented Spanish dancer) were also friends of my mother and possibly distant cousins. Emilio, a Quaker, was one of the nicest human beings I ever met and one of the most talented.

H. Emilio Osta.

M. Teresita Osta.

Later in 1950 Juan almost made a movie, a musical comedy entitled "Gypsy Caravan," in the U.S. He had accumulated a number of studio 78 rpm records as well as a tape recording of the music as well as reams of sheet music of the various pieces. The script for this proposed project may have been partially based on the material he used in 1934-1936 as his Spanish dance troupe toured Spain. The music this time was his own, not Francisco Avellan's. A financier by the name of Callahan backed the project. A number of musicians and actors had been hired, rehearsals had started, and then Mr. Callahan changed his mind and pulled the plug.

After 1950s' "Crisis" Juan didn't have a lot of movie parts that I remember. Here's a list of all the movies he ever made to my knowledge. Few of these movies have survived and the rest are known only to movie historians or old people with long memories.

Flying Down to Rio
The Cossacks (Fox)
The Feathered Serpent (Charlie Chan)
Codigo Penal (The Criminal Code)
*Paris de Noche* (Paris at Night)
The Man from Montreal
A Message to Garcia
*Los Que Danzan* (Those Who Dance)
*Cascarabias*
*Amor Audaz* (Audacious Love)
*30 Segundos de Vida* (Mexico) (30 Seconds of Love)
One Mad Kiss
Tango
Mr. Moto on the Island
Fury of the Jungle
The Victim
El Apache
Storm Over the Andes
Black Fury (starring Paul Muni)
Grumpy
On the Great White Trail
The Palomino
The Loves of Carmen (starring Rita Hayworth)

Crisis (starring Cary Grant)
The Razor's Edge (starring Tyrone Power)
Daughter of the West (he had a small part and co-authored the
music score with Victor Granados)
A Night at the Opera (starring Groucho Marx)

Juan in "A Message to Garcia."

**Juan in "A Message to Garcia."**

During 1951 we visited some of Juan's friends in the Spanish entertainment community. One evening we went to dinner at the Beverly Hills home of Amparo and Jose Iturbi (brother and sister world-famous concert pianists). Amparo even played for us after dinner.

This is the year we visited Juan's friend Señor Wences the famous Spanish ventriloquist in his West Los Angeles house. Señor Wences (whose legal name was Wenceslao Moreno) also had an apartment in New York where he made frequent appearances on the Ed Sullivan television show.

Wences and Juan.

Wences' house was typical of the many Spanish style homes built in West Los Angeles in the twenties and thirties. It even had a small enclosed patio in front with a fountain.

One evening that same year we had dinner
with Juan's friend Martin Garralaga and his wife.

Tripe (cow's stomach) was on the menu. Well, the old expression, "It would gag a maggot," was applicable. However, I bravely ate it, making neither complaint nor facial grimace that would have given away the game. For this bravado acting performance I was given great praise by Juan and my mother on the way home. Manners and courtesy are highly valued in Spanish culture. They are even "built in" to the structure and grammar of the language itself.

One of the famous Spanish composers of the 19th century was Enrique Granados. Juan was a friend of Enrique's son Victor, and collaborated with him on various songs and on the musical score for the movie "Daughter of the West." I met Victor briefly when Juan visited him at his apartment in Hollywood.

In 1952 Juan left a spec script entitled, *Corrida De Toros* ("Bullfight"), about a boy and a fighting bull with the King Brothers, well-known Hollywood independent producers, using an intermediary, "Mr. Gould," who came to our house to pick up the script. I have a memory of briefly meeting Mr. Gould and thinking he was a nice man. I was ten. I was to be proven right!

I remember that Juan, in summarizing the plot of the script for my mother and I, said that it had to do with a boy who raises a fighting bull from which he is separated but meets later in the bullring where he fights so bravely he is given an *Indulto*, (a "pardon") and where they recognize each other to the amazement of the crowd.

Some of Juan's friends in Hollywood in those days weren't even actors. I remember him talking about one such person, Bill Clothier. He was a top cinematographer of his day with credits such as "Rio Lobo" and "Donovan's Reef." Another actor friend of Juan's was Joseph Calleia.

These photographs of Juan were taken around 1952 just before he became ill with cancer.

Father Junipero Serra, founder of the Spanish missions of California, was one of the historical personages he admired, along with Fray Bartolome de Las Casas (a champion of early Indian rights) and Santa Teresa de Avila (a Spanish mystic).

In 1953 Juan was diagnosed with cancer and despite treatment at the VA Hospital on Sawtelle in West Los Angeles it spread. Towards the end he sought treatment with a Doctor Harris who was using laetrile obtained in Mexico. The metastasis continued and Juan died at the VA Hospital on April 1, 1954, and was buried at the nearby VA cemetery on Sawtelle.

In his last days at the hospital he was still cogent and liked by the staff there because he was courteous and endured his last days patiently and without complaint. He received the Last Sacraments of his church and was said to have seen a vision of Jesus Christ coming to welcome him just before he died.

Juan's writing of "Corrida," "Gypsy Caravan," and in defending Blasco Ibañez's novel from "cultural castration" were all efforts to bridge the cultural gap between Hispanic/Latinos and Anglos, between the Spanish and English-speaking worlds.

# 5

## Juan's Legacy

Late in 1954 we moved into Señor Wences' house in West Los Angeles—at his urging. Of course Wences did not live there much of the time. He traveled frequently back and forth between the U.S. and Europe. Señor Wences was as astute as he was generous. He made my mother believe she was doing him a favor by moving into his house and taking care of it for him. He well understood Spanish pride. Had he made the offer as an act of charity it would have been rejected. And I would have lost the opportunity to grow up in a lovely home in a quiet, secure neighborhood. It was near the La Brea Tar Pits and I once dug up in the garden what I'm sure was a fossil hoof of Eohypus (Dawn Horse) or something similar.

Señor Wences' generosity was partially paid back because my mother was an awesome cook. When he spent a couple weeks with us she would cook up a storm (Spanish food, American food, etc.). Since Wences traveled so much he was fond of home cooking and just relaxing. And he treated us as if we were family.

Señor Wences' wife, Taly (Natalia), only accompanied him on one visit to our house. She was a very straightforward person and told us she despised the West Coast (and loved New York). When she discovered my mother was the same kind of no-nonsense straightforward person they hit it off right away. She and my mother communicated ever after by phone or letter as needed and were on good terms. Taly was good to me as well. She was a woman of culture and intelligence and helped Wences with his career.

Wences preferred Los Angeles to New York. At that time Los Angeles still retained a bit of its early Spanish influences; our neighborhood was quiet, scenic, and peaceful. And my mother's paella and roast lamb were memorable.

When Wences was home, his "friends," Johnny, Pedro and Cecilia

Chicken came along to visit. If Señor Wences was in the mood we would get an impromptu show at the dinner table. At breakfast, if a hardboiled egg was handy, Cecilia Chicken might put in an appearance.

So I would have a memento of these visits Señor Wences gave me professional photographs of Johnny, Pedro and Cecilia Chicken.

Johnny.

Señor Wences and Pedro.

**Señor Wences and Cecilia Chicken.**

The photo below is Wences and Johnny taken at the Ed Sullivan Show, possibly by his wife, Taly. He has annotated it with his characteristic warm and quirky style, "With three hugs, Wences."

Wences and Johnny.

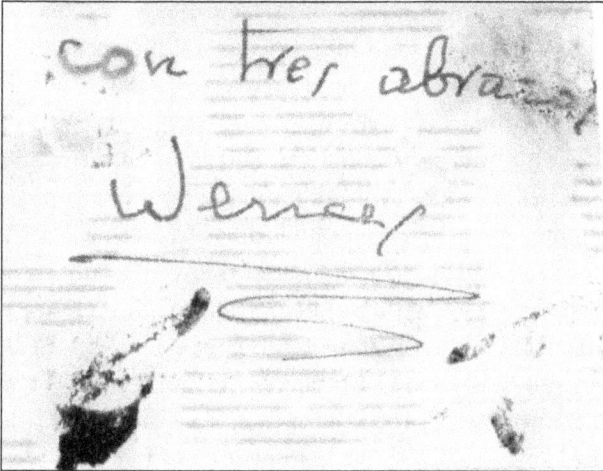

"With three hugs, Wences".

In 1956 the King Brothers, Maurice and Frank, produced a movie entitled, "The Brave One." This movie was about a poor Mexican country boy named Leonardo who raises a fighting bull "Gitano" (Gypsy) as his personal pet; a gift from Don Alejandro the ranch owner. Leonardo's father saved Don Alejandro's niece from serious injury and Gitano was the reward! Leonardo and Gitano grew up together, then one day Don Alejandro is killed in a car accident and the greedy and nasty ranch manager claims Leonardo has no legal ownership paper for Gitano. Gitano is put in with the other bulls and is sent to the city for the next bullfight. Meanwhile, Leonardo visits El Presidente in his palace and gets a pardon for Gitano. Leonardo rushes off to the bullring only to find Gitano gone from the holding pen. But Gitano has fought so bravely that the audience yells, "Indulto!" And as the judges spare Gitano's life, Leonardo jumps into the ring to the horror of the audience. They are amazed when the bull stops his charge at the last moment and Leonardo hugs him. A real sentimental crowd-pleaser!

If you analyze the above plot and strip it down to its bare essentials, it sounds something like what Juan orally described to my mother and me in the spec script that he turned over to the King Brothers in 1952. There are differences, for one, "Corrida" was set in Spain, the origin of bullfighting. The "Brave One" was set in Mexico. In "Corrida" the young man was starting a career as a bullfighter. In "Brave One" he was a child, reclaiming his pet and stolen property. Yet on a conceptual level they were both a "boy and his pet bull—and their chance meeting in later years."

The above minimum facts about "Corrida" are from my memory. I never read the script—either then or later. I don't know how Juan's plot dealt with the "Indulto." My limited knowledge of bullfighting etiquette suggests the bull would have to fight bravely to earn it. Therefore, did the young bullfighter have to fight his own pet bull? This plot twist would not appeal to American audiences! It might have to a Spanish audience (if neither bull or bullfighter died). Another plot option would be the bull proving his bravery by goring the featured bullfighter of the day—and the young torero was sent in as a replacement. If Juan's plot had either option, I cannot see the Kings liking it.

Two amazing things happened the next year (1957). The movie "The Brave One" won an Academy Award for Best Screenplay from an Original Source; it's what's known in the movie business as a "sleeper hit." Secondly, Robert Rich, the alleged author, did not show up to pick up his Oscar! Nor did anyone else. This might have been the only time in the movie business that such a strange thing happened. The Oscar was to stay unclaimed until 1975!

At first the Kings claimed "Robert Rich" wrote the screenplay. In 1957 Dell Comics published *The Brave One* (Issue 773) (from which the above plot synopsis was taken) and gave screenplay credit to Harry Franklin and Merrill G. White.

As time went on Robert Rich was found to be a nephew of the Kings, but he adamantly denied writing the script. In fact, he was interviewed by the FBI (Report, File 100-138754, Serial #1118, Part 13 of 15) the day after the King Bros. Oscar was not picked up. Probably because of the Hollywood rumor that Dalton Trumbo authored "The Brave One." Although Rich admitted to being the "go-between" for the King Bros. dealings with Trumbo (passing money and scripts back and forth) no script with the name "The Brave One" did he admit to handling.

After nearly two years of controversy in the press, the claim was finally forwarded that Dalton Trumbo had been the author. Trumbo claimed to have written both the original story and the screenplay.

In late 1958 or early 1959, within weeks after the "Trumbo Authorship Claim" was advanced, my mother went on Los Angeles television on "Confidential File" with investigative reporter, Paul Coates, to explain how Juan had given a spec script to the King Brothers and how she believed they had stolen Juan's story idea to make "The Brave One."

Trumbo was of course controversial because he was one of Hollywood's "blacklisted" authors who refused to answer questions of HUAC (The House Un-American Activities Committee). For that reason, the King Bros. had wanted to keep his authorship hidden as was common practice in those days.

In Paul Coates' "Confidential File" *Los Angeles Times* column of January 22, 1959, it's related that Eugene Gould, a significant stockholder in King Brothers Productions, was the person that took Juan's "Corrida De Toros" script, after having read it and liked it, to the King Brothers in 1952 (thus confirming my memory of events).

When Mr. Gould picked up the script a week later (from the Kings), Maury said he didn't like it but some time later Frank told him their next production would be "The Boy and the Bull." Gould's final response in the Coates interview was, "But if 'The Brave One' was from Juan Duval's original story, I see no reason why I should hide anything to keep him from getting credit."

Documentation is always paramount in a legal case but so are solid witnesses. As witnesses go, Mr. Gould would have been a "ringer." A "ringer" witness is not enough to win a lawsuit. In 1959, my mother filed suit against the King Bros. Within a few months she accepted a settlement ($15,000, I believe);

a fair piece of change in those days. Having accepted the settlement, she was precluded from seeking the Oscar on Juan's behalf.

My mother's settlement was put to good use fueling the economy, as windfalls to the poor usually do. The first thing she did was to treat the both of us to a bus tour of several of the national parks of the West. Next, she bought a Ford Fairlane 500, the first and last car she ever bought in her life. With the remainder she helped finance my college education.

So, what happened back in 1952? I don't know and I'm fairly sure we will never know. All the documents are lost and the adult participants (I was ten at the time) are probably deceased. When I was younger I was suspicious of "coincidence" but as I grew older I was astonished when "coincidence" happened to me. So, I accept it's possible that the King Bros. and Dalton Trumbo developed "The Brave One" without any reference whatsoever to Juan's "Corrida" script. Bullfighting was a hot topic in those days (as indicated by the earlier references to "Blood and Sand" and "The Loves of Carmen").

I also know more about the way movies are made, both in Hollywood and elsewhere. Scripts are often developed when producers/directors talk to their "favored" script writers and pitch some ideas to them. (The writer in these situations assumes the ideas pitched are the intellectual property of the producer.) Then the writer will do a "spec" script or maybe just a "Treatment." The Kings could have challenged Trumbo by saying, "Can you write us a script about a boy and his pet bull and have them meet in a bullring years later?" Since the Kings knew Trumbo had been to Mexico recently, was interested in bullfighting, and was an accomplished writer that would have been all that was needed to produce "The Brave One." Such a scenario is possible. But this is supposition only; I know of no facts that support it. Because something is plausible doesn't mean it happened.

I also believe it's possible for people to do things they are consciously unaware of, such as borrowing an "idea" which you can consider a piece of a plot. The Kings could have consciously disliked Juan's script but unconsciously liked and maybe borrowed an idea from it. Like my stepfather, I too have read Carl Jung.

When Dalton Trumbo said he wrote the original story and the final script for "The Brave One," I believe him. I believe he acted in good faith—and I believe he deserved the Oscar he won for "The Brave One." My favorite of all the movies he scripted was "Thirty Seconds Over Tokyo" (the story of the Doolittle Raid on Tokyo early in the war).

I'm sorry that the King Bros. and Trumbo had to work at making movies clandestinely. It is not a period in our history we should be proud of. Have politicians learned not to use the FBI as a cat's paw to blunt political dissent? It seems to me the FBI could have gotten all the information they needed from Hedda Hopper or some other gossip columnist at vastly lower cost to taxpayers. I think Robert Rich would have agreed with me.

This photograph taken in 1959 shows the front room of Señor Wences' house in West Los Angeles. Seated on the left is Señor Wences and my mother on the right. (I don't remember the name of the gentleman seated in the middle.) From the left (standing) is myself, Mr. Lazaro Bartolome, who was a friend of Wences and an ex-diplomat with the Spanish Consul, and Armando Moreno (Wences' son) and his wife, visiting from Argentina.

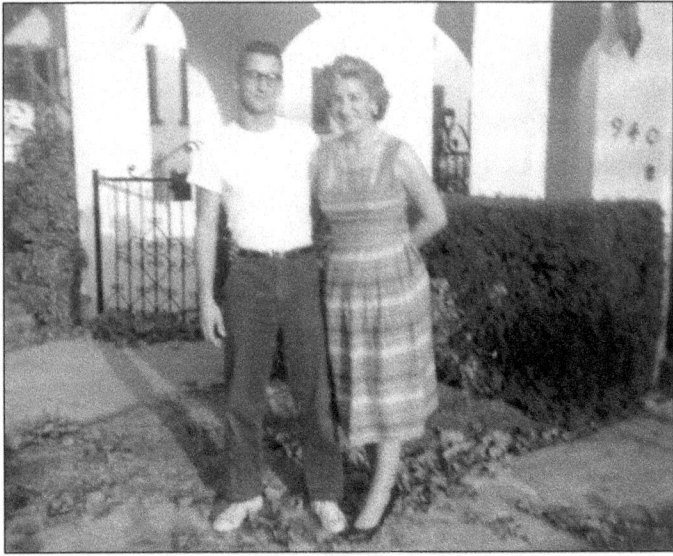

My mother and me in 1959, standing in front of Wences' house.

My mother never loved another man after Juan. He was a "tough act to follow." The widow had offers, both of love and marriage, but declined.

My mother didn't move out of Señor Wences' house until 1970. He never asked her to leave, God bless him, but a joint friend of ours and Señor Wences told her she should let him have a chance to enjoy Wences' house and generosity. Spanish pride told her it was time to leave, so she did. Besides, all her family was now in Northern California so she moved back to San Francisco to a residential hotel. Later we were able to help her move to a better location in Berkeley.

As the years passed, my mother and I and Wences sometimes exchanged Christmas cards.

Felices Pascuas
y
Año Nueva
with best wishes
for all the days of
the coming year

SEÑOR WENCES

This card shows Wences with his grandson. I often wish I had kept some of his other cards because he often did excellent humorous drawings and doodles just as Juan used to do. To multi-talented people the ability to draw seems to be a common talent.

As the years went by I realized one of the gifts Juan had given me was his model of what it is to be a gentleman.

What is my definition of a gentleman? Someone who treats all people equally and respectfully be they VIPs or peasants, rich or poor, famous or unknown; someone with good manners and someone who is generous to family and friends. Someone who tries hard to communicate with everyone around him, even those he does not understand or like. It's also been called "civility" and by looking at political dialogue in America today, has almost disappeared. Nor can our children remember to say "please" or "thank you;" they are too busy being spoiled little princes and princesses.

Juan had a favorite Spanish proverb: *Dime con quien andas y te digo que eres* ("Tell me who you hang around with and I'll tell you what you are"). Then there was *De noche todos los gatos son pardos* ("At night all cats are grey"). And *Lo mas se revuelve, mas huele,* ("The more you stir it the more it smells").

Here are some of his favorite toasts: *Ahoga el demonio!* ("Drown the Devil!"). It's what you say to your host when you are holding out an empty glass asking for a refill. Then there's *Salud y pesetas, y tiempo para gastarlas!* ("Health and money, and time to spend the money!"). Spaniards, like the British, appreciate a wry sense of humor.

I think the first of the above proverbs when applied to Juan's own life works very well. Many of his friends such as Manuel de Falla, Emilio Osta, and Señor Wences were gentlemen of the Old School. De Falla I know only through history books. The other two I knew fairly well over a period of many years.

In January 1990, my mother died at age 79. I sent Señor Wences a copy of the funeral/obituary notice. Wences was born one year before Juan (in 1896) so he would have been 94 at the time. He responded with a gracious note of condolence which reflected what a true gentleman and caballero he was.

**Note from Wences.**

Here is a translation of Señor Wences' letter:

Marbella, February 27, 1990
Dear Friend Jose:
With sorrow I received your letter giving me the fatal notice of the death of your dear mother (Rest in Peace).
If you want anything from us, just ask. A kiss for your son and greetings to your wife and for your mother, in addition to my prayer I have my tears.
Hugs from Wences and Taly

I had my own tears nine years later upon hearing of Wences' death at the age of 103! He was *un caballero muy distinguido!*

At the beginning of the new millennium my worst fear was that Juan's name and particularly his music and writings would disappear without a trace. All of his stories, screenplays, and sheet music had been lost.

In 2000 I took all of Juan's "demo" records and the tape made by Emilio Osta to a sound studio where they worked them up into a CD.

This one-hour CD is entitled, *Musica de Juan Duval-Juan Bellavista Xicart-Gypsy Caravan* ("Spanish Soul Music"). This was put together from studio 78 recordings of the 1930s and 1940s and a single tape recording of the ballet *El Zapaterito"* None of the music Juan co-authored with Victor Granados is included.

A number of the individual pieces of the CD are vocals in English; humorous movie musical material (from the failed "Gypsy Caravan" project). Most are instrumentals and imbued with Gypsy flavor and vivacity, but are not traditional *Cante Hondo.* Some are lively and melodic, others more intense and complex. Most pieces are the equal of the well-known 19th and 20th century Spanish composers, in my opinion. I'm no music expert but I have often listened to this music in a two-record set of Spanish music recorded by my pianist cousin Emilio Osta.

There are fourteen compositions of various lengths on the CD:

1. A Day in June (1:31)
2. La Gitana Del Puerto (3:28)
3. A Call of Love (3:200)

4. We are the Wandering Gypsies (3:20)
5. *Sacromonte* (4:33)
6. Divine Land of Paradise (4:20)
7. Confused (3:15)
8. All My Life I've Been a Victim (3:20)
9. Finale (2:49)
10. *Las Lavanderas* ("The Washerwomen") (3:28)
11. Cantata, Part 1 (3:30)
12. Cantata, Part 2 (3:21)
13. Life is an Open Book (4:20)
14. *El Zapaterito* ("The Little Cobbler"), ballet (16:35)

Most of these pieces were recorded by different musicians at inexpensive music studios and most were 78s from the 1930s and 1940s. I don't know if Juan did any of the piano work but I know he did some of the castanets and heelwork. In the forties Juan was just beginning to make a Hollywood movie entitled "Gypsy Caravan," but funding collapsed at the last minute when the major financial backer pulled out. It was to be a musical comedy with songs in English having lovely and mostly happy melodies throughout.

The first piece on the CD is aptly named. It is a lively and happy mix of piano and castanets. The second is a mix of piano, castanets, and guitar that are quintessentially Spanish. This is my favorite. The guitar work was done by Geronimo Villarino who was a good friend of Juan's and a talented artist. The third piece is a haunting piano serenade, quiet and melodic.

The fourth is a lively, clever, and humorous tune with several vocalists. Gypsy musical comedy—lots of fun! Fifth is a combination of piano and footwork. Stately, but still lively. Sixth is a romantic duet with Trini and Felipe. Trini's voice and range is spectacular. Seventh is Trini's love lament—sweet and melodic. The eighth is a melodic piano piece. Ninth is a compelling piano piece with some finishing flourishes. Tenth is piano with some female vocalists singing a humorous lament. The words here are hard to understand but the music is bouncy and is accompanied by "washtub noises" (not provided by the musicians or singers but by the fact this vinyl record sustained damage from storage and old age).

The eleventh piece is piano work with a brooding stately, almost Moorish feeling (a bit like Cante Hondo). Twelve is a continuation of the themes of #11 but with more melodic development. Thirteen is piano with male and female gypsy vocalists—and more humor.

Fourteen is special. It is the longest piece, was composed last, and has an interesting history. It is also Juan's attempt as a composer to move beyond musical comedy tunes into the "symphonic." Did he succeed? Listen and find out. Mostly, it is piano work with castanets. Haunting motifs are introduced, then repeated. In the middle there is a stepped-up pace—torrero music. Then a vocal duet and recurring melodic themes.

As was mentioned earlier, this piece was tape recorded at the home of cowboy star John McIntyre. If you have a quick ear, you will hear two tiny blips of sound in the beginning where "party noise" was mostly "clipped off" at the recording studio. Emilio's rendering of this piece "at first sight" is a tour de force endorsement of his skill.

A word of warning to those who have never listened to old "aural history" (prior to the digital age). Be aware this music has lots of 'hissing,' 'washtub noises,' etc. associated with early technology. Rest assured the beauty of this music shines through the miasma. I once had a Caruso record—it was a time machine link to another era—and was very sad when it became unlistenable.

Emilio Osta of Spanish and Basque ancestry, started out as a child prodigy. He received his formal training under Gyula Ormay then with renowned virtuosi Josef Lhevinne and Leopold Godowsky. He made a world concert tour in his twenties and became a recognized interpreter of Iberian and Latin-American music for the piano.

Emilio knew my mother and was a friend of Juan's. Emilio's talented sister Teresita was a Spanish dancer who was a close friend of my mother's. This linkup of people was due to La Union Española of San Francisco, which was a typical immigrant organization providing cultural continuity as people became assimilated into the broader culture. That's 'where and how' my mother and Juan met.

Emilio's two recordings (33s) of regional Spanish music are probably still well known to music historians. Regiones De Espana (AO 1082) features Madrid/Granada/Navarra, including Turina's Sacromonte. The fifth track on Juan's CD is his version of Sacromonte. (Sacromonte is the Sacred Mountain of the Gypsies.) Emilio's second recording is also titled Regiones De Espana VIR-CAP Records (COV 206104), manufactured by Action Records, San Mateo, California. Regions here are "Andalucia," "Vasconia" (the Basque Country) and Castilla.

Emilio was Juan's friend—but he also became mine—over a very long time-span. He married late in life and both my wife and I met his charming wife Tulia in their home in Tucson. Emilio achieved success in educational TV with his "Great Composers for Piano" which ran four years on the University of Arizona station KUAT-TV, and in Phoenix and Albuquerque, New Mexico. He was also a music professor at that university. Emilio was talented, charming and a true caballero.

Of course, copyright on all of the above-referenced music and literary works mentioned herein has expired and is in the public domain. Use it as you please; keep it alive!

I made copies of this CD and passed them around to various people including a musical historian of Spanish music, a performing Spanish guitarist, and a music promoter.

None of these efforts yielded any positive results so by 2010 I thought the entire world neither knew nor cared about Juan Duval. Life had a further surprise. One day my granddaughter, Samantha Bonelli, told me there was a website on the Internet that memorialized my stepfather, and that there was a John Duval who claimed Juan Duval was his father! What a stunning surprise that was.

Juan had never spoken of having fathered any children or having been married at some earlier time in his life. Of course, gentlemen are discreet and don't discuss their prior amours. He had always treated me as his son, leaving me (in a written will) all the rights to his music. In a way he saw me as his successor who would continue his work—as a pianist and hopefully as a composer. He even "gave" me his music, telling me to put my name on it. I humored him on all this, acceding as children must when grownups press them. Besides, I could see how sick he was, and near death.

Even at ten I knew (Spanish pride again) I could not do such a dishonorable thing as put my name to someone else's artistic accomplishment. It sounded like stealing to me back then. It still does. There's a time to speak up and a time to be silent. I said nothing for it would have hurt the step-father who loved me as if I were his own flesh and blood; who used his GI Bill Educational Benefits to have a professional piano teacher give me lessons in piano and counterpoint.

It's an old-world tradition for a father to teach his son his trade. Juan could play the piano and was a composer. He had a vast array of other artistic skills. Musically speaking, I'm a dunce, but I was smart and even at ten years of age it was obvious to me I had less musical talent than a dung beetle. Something neither my mother nor Juan could see.

At first I was dubious of this John Duval "mystery man" from my past. Suddenly I had a "step-brother" or whatever you call someone with this relationship to you. I made phone contact first then visited him in person. And as he told me more details of his past, I became convinced he was who he said he was. He knew the kind of inside details that only someone who had been there sixty years ago would know. He appears to have some of the talents Juan had as well.

According to John, his mother had met Juan in San Francisco at the Opera House. He was conceived in Mill Valley in September 1947. At that time I was living with my mother and father on Clay Street in San Francisco's Chinatown. We would not meet for 63 years!

Juan did not know he had fathered a child until he was on his deathbed and John's mother went to visit him at the Veteran's Hospital, asking his permission to allow her to give his surname to her son, which he of course agreed to, as any gentleman would.

A strong bond now unites John Duval and myself; we are both eager that Juan's life and accomplishments be better known; he with his website and me with the writing of Juan's biography.

In October of 2006, my wife and I visited Spain and spent some days seeing the beauties of Barcelona—including a visit to Montserrat. We saw what Juan hoped and longed for—a democratic and prosperous Catalonia and Spain.

Time flies—and I have not heard from John for several years. I suspect he has passed; he had told me of a serious medical problem. His last letter to me was dated July 11, 2013. He had moved permanently to France in hopes of obtaining dual citizenship in the country in which his father had passed many productive years.

My final wish for Juan's memory is that some music conservatory in his native Catalonia will hear the beauty of Juan's music and preserve it for posterity. And play it at the *Palau de la Musica Catalana*!

# Selected References

Alpert, Michael. *A New International History of the Spanish Civil War*. United Kingdom: Paul Graves MacMillan, 2004.

Bauer, Carlos. *Cries From a Wounded Madrid: Poetry of the Spanish Civil War*. Athens, Ohio: Swallow Press, 1984.

Beevor, Anthony. *The Battle for Spain: The Spanish Civil War 1936–1939*. New York: Penguin, 2006.

Davis, Paul K. *100 Decisive Battles from Ancient Times to the Present*. Oxford: Oxford University Press, 2001.

Forester, C.S. *The Gun*. New York: Bantam Pathfinder, 1966.

Gibson, Ian. *Federico Garcia Lorca, A Life*. New York: Knopf Doubleday Publishing Group, 1997.

Kropotkin, Princess Alexandra. Translators Preface. *War and Peace*. New York: Nelson Doubleday, 1960.

Maltin, Leonard. *Leonard Maltin's Movie Guide, 2007 Edition*. New York: Penguin Group, 2006.

Mayhew, J. *The Princeton Encyclopedia of Poetry and Poetics*. Princeton: Princeton University Press, 2012.

Thomas, Hugh. *The Spanish Civil War*. New York: Harper and Row, 1961.